For Aspiring Producers, Writers, Musicians, Singers, and Future Record Moguls

# Brian Wesley Peters

Designed by Terry Ogram Barnes

First Edition

Swerve Publishing, Los Angeles, California

## DISCLAIMER

This book is designed to provide information on the music business. It is sold with the understanding that the publisher and author are not engaged in rendering legal, accounting, or other professional services. If legal or other expert assistance is required, the services of a competent professional should be sought.

It is not the purpose of this manual to reprint all the information that is otherwise available to anyone trying to enter into the music business, but instead to complement, amplify, and support other texts. You are urged to read all the available material, learn as much as possible about the music business, and tailor the Information to your individual needs.

Every effort has been made to make this manual as complete and as accurate as possible. However, there *may be mistakes*, both in typography and content. Therefore, this text should be used only as a general guide and not as the ultimate source of information on the music business. This manual contains information on the music business that is current only up to the printing date.

The purpose of this manual is to educate and entertain. The author and Swerve Publishing shall have neither liability nor responsibility to any person or entity with respect to any loss or damage caused, or alleged to have been caused, directly or indirectly, by the information contained in this book.

If you do not wish to be bound by the above, you may return this book to the publisher for a full refund.

# FOREWORD

From his beginnings as a teenage "wonder-boy" with an eye for spotting talent, to becoming a record company owner himself, and accomplishing many other things in so few years, Brian Peters is one of the most instinctively gifted people I have known and had the pleasure of working with in the music business.

Being a product of the "instant age" of fast foods, e-mails, the Internet, and overnight delivery, Brian has accomplished the feat of creating a kind of "quick reference guide" for the music business enthusiast. This book zips you through the record-making process, all the way from production to distribution. It delves through the very latest technological playing fields of digital entertainment, and covers the territory of daunting legal challenges.

Brian Peters has managed to pack over 18 years of his knowledge of and experience in the music business into the pages of this book. Overall, the reader will find this a perfect source for answers to frequently asked questions on the Hows, Whys, Whens, Wheres, and Whats of the music business. The answers can be found right here.

> —*Jerry Peters*
> *Grammy award-winning producer, composer, arranger,*
> *and songwriter for artists including Luther Vandross,*
> *Whitney Houston, Natalie Cole, Marvin Gaye, Patti Labelle,*
> *and many others*

2118 Wilshire Boulevard
Suite 1040
Santa Monica, CA 90403

Copyright © 2005 Swerve Publishing

ISBN: 0-9768289-0-1
Publisher's Cataloging-In-Publication Data
(Prepared by The Donohue Group, Inc.)

Peters, Brian Wesley.
Music business 101 : a guide to understanding the music business /
Brian Wesley Peters ; designed by Terry Barnes. -- 1st ed. --

p. ; cm.
Includes index.
ISBN: 0-9768289-0-1

1. Popular music--Writing and publishing. 2. Music trade--United States--Marketing--
Handbooks, manuals, etc. 3. Music publishing--United States--Handbooks, manuals, etc.
4. Sound recording industry--United States--Handbooks, manuals, etc. 5. Music trade--
United States--Vocational guidance. I. Barnes, Terry. II. Title.

ML3790 .P48 2005
780.68/8

Edited by Gail M. Kearns, To Press and Beyond, Santa Barbara, California
Cover design by Russell Robinson
Book design by Terry Barnes Design, Sherman Oaks, California

Printed in the United States of America

## ACKNOWLEDGMENTS

First of all I would like to thank my Lord and Savior Jesus Christ for giving me the ability to create this book. I would like to thank my son Micah who has been my inspiration for writing this book. I would also like to thank several people who assisted me at various stages of this creative process. To my mother, Regina Peters, who helped during the editing process: Thank you for your patience and for working gratis. To my Auntie Rhoda, who accepted all my calls during my time of need. I am also grateful for the support of my father, Theodore Peters, and my brothers, Eric and Corey. Thanks to my friends: Nicole Restivo, Bridgette Morgan, Professor James Roberson, Rashidi Harper, Walter Milsap III, Page E. Turner, Terence Smith, Gorden Campbell, Reggie Bufkin, and Azul Cruz. Thanks for all your input, contributions, and patience in listening to my stories about this book. Thanks to all my immediate family, my extended family, and for my Greater Liberty Church Family—with special thanks to Barbara Doss.

A special thank you to my uncle, Jerry Peters, who taught me everything I know about the music business. He has been a great example in my life, professionally and spiritually. To Gail Kearns, of To Press and Beyond: Thank you for your patience and hard work. To Terry McFadden: Thank you for your advice; you never knew you inspired me to write a book. To Terry Barnes: You have inspired and pushed me beyond my expectations; without you this book would not have been possible.

Thanks to Jheryl Busby, Skip Scarbrough, Charles Veal, and all of the musicians, artist/performers, producers, and musical talents who have influenced, encouraged, and inspired me along the way.

To my business partners, George Hambrick and Joseph Wolfe: Thank you for the opportunity to learn so much about this business that I love so much.

INTRODUCTION

When I first had the idea of writing a book about the record business, there were already several books on the subject. But as I began to look into them, I realized most were written by attorneys and accountants, and you practically needed a law degree to read them.

That's when I realized there was a need for a simple, easy-to-understand, straight-to-the-point description of how the record business really works. Why do you need this? Because if you're considering a career in music, what you don't know will definitely cost you.

This book addresses topics and questions people have asked me throughout my years in the business—questions that are as important now as they were 75 years ago, when the record business was in its infancy.

What you are about to read is a description of the record business as it has been for about the last 50 years. But the Internet is changing everything, and part of this book is dedicated to outlining changes that may benefit you most.

—*Brian Wesley Peters*

## DEDICATION

This book is dedicated to the memory of my loving Auntie, Pauline Vance, who always encouraged me to keep going strong and to pursue all my dreams.

And to my darling son, Micah, this book is dedicated to you. This is what I did during the tough times I was apart from you.

CONTENTS

ence CD • Pressing • Soundtrack • Cover tune • Album snippets • Logo • Five quick tips for improving your mixdown masters • Timeline of current media technology • Vinyl • Cassette • Compact Disc • DAT • Minidisc • Audio DVD • Music as digital code • WAVE, AIFF files • MP3 and MP4 • How music goes from concept to recorded product

## 3   Contracts: For Better or For Worse                61

What is a contract? • Recording contract basics • Basic disagreements that lead to agreements • What is the Seven-Year Rule? • Everyone says I should read the contract... • Is your attorney worth $300 an hour? • Don't think "demo" • Can't I just get a copy of the form and fill it in? • The nuts and bolts of a recording contract negotiation • Contract • License • Negotiation • What other kinds of contracts might be needed? • Producer's contract • Production deal agreement • What is a "Key Man" clause? • Imprint deal • Joint venture • Can an artist showcase help get a recording deal? • Please listen to my demo • Master purchase deal • What can a logo do for me? • How are recording contracts negotiated? • Work for hire • Re-recording restrictions • Exclusive • Recoupment • Points • Sides • A-side protection • Entertainment law • Music contract software and Websites • Booking agreement • Assignment of copyright • Artist/manager agreement • Co-publishing agreement • Joint venture agreement

## 4   Ins and Outs of Music Publishing              85

Licensing • How do songs earn royalties? • Mechanical license • Statutory license • Co-publishing agreement • What is a license? • How a song's royalties are divided • Shared copyright • Mechanical license • Sampling made simple • Obtaining a sample clearance • Clearing samples yourself • How to clear a sample • Transfer of copyrights • What is sheet music? • Why is it called a "mechanical license"? • Who needs sheet music? • Types of sheet music • How a mechanical license works • Mechanical license statutory royalty rates • How do I get a mechanical license? • To obtain copyright forms • Statutory license • Controlled composition • The Harry Fox Agency, Inc. • Copyright • How does a copyright help me? • Radio stations pay for the music they play • How to copyright your music • The poor man's copyright • Public domain • Work for hire • Copyright collective • All three performance rights organizations pay pretty much the same … • Performance rights organizations • BMI • ASCAP • When music is performed in public … • SESAC • What can a music publisher do for me? • Other organizations you need to know about • RIAA • NARAS • NARM • NARM conventions • AFIM • MIDEM • How a copyright works • Sample clearance form • How music generates royalties

## 5   Songwriting and Song Placement              111

Artist and repertoire • Digital songwriting tools • Copyright notice • What is a musical score? • Musical score • Writer breakdown • Composer • Different styles of songwriting • Rhythm and blues • Hip-hop • Pop • What does the copyist do? • Jazz • Gospel • Classical music • Melody • Lyrics • Songwriter • Singer/Songwriter • Film score • The metronome • Film composer • Soundtrack • Modern orchestra seating chart

# 1.

# Distributors and Distribution

Distribution is how recorded music goes from stacks of finished product through a series of middlemen and into the consumers' hands. The distributor buys the product at a wholesale price from the record label and re-sells it at a higher price to record stores (**retailers**), who in turn re-sell it to consumers at or near the suggested retail list price (**SRLP**). The distributor's job is to get orders from the music buyers at chains, racks, and one-stops. The distributor gets orders through its staff of sales reps and by mailing **sales solicitations** (**one-sheets**) for each new album to retailers coast–to–coast.

Distributors have two other critical functions: inventory control (warehousing records) and billing to and collecting from their stores. When a sales rep gets an order, it is passed to the warehouse, where it is filled and shipped. Large distributors have enormous warehouses—up to a million square feet —with sophisticated, robotic inventory control systems that allow them to ship most orders the same day.

The **preorder** process ensures that stores everywhere receive new product and make it available to consumers almost immediately. Timing is crucial to distributors and record labels. They want to manufacture all the records the stores will need at one time, and compete for the highest entry or bullets on *Billboard* charts.

**Preorders** are coordinated by the label's and distributors' sales reps. Each rep is assigned specific accounts to solicit (request) for orders on new

## Who are the four major record distributors?

**UNI** (Universal, Interscope/A&M, MCA, Motown, Island/Def Jam, Geffen, Mercury, DreamWorks)
Owner: Vivendi (France)

**Sony BMG** (Sony, 550, Arista, Columbia, Epic, J, Jive, LaFace, RCA)
Owners: Sony 50% (Japan), Bertelsmann AG 50% (Germany)

**WEA** (Warner Elektra Atlantic, Bad Boy, Elektra, Lava, Maverick, Nonesuch, Reprise, Rhino, Sire, Warner Bros. Word, Warner Music International)
Owner: Warner Music Group (U.S.)

**EMD** (Capitol, Virgin, Priority, EMI Christian, Angel, Blue Note, Chrysalis)
Owner: EMI-Capitol Music Group (U.K.)

## Why so many different prices?

*U.S. retailers can sell records at any price they wish. The **SRLP** (suggested retail list price) is the price stores are expected to assign a record, minus special discounts. SRLP is also the price record labels use to calculate artist and producer royalties. It is roughly twice the **wholesale price** (the price paid by middlemen and record retailers). The average new album's SRLP is between $11.98 and $16.98, so it sells to record stores for $5.98–$8.98. The lowest wholesale prices are reserved for **mass merchants** (Best Buy Target, Wal-Mart, etc.) that buy the largest quantities. After all, selling 100 records to 1,000 different accounts is much more work than selling 100,000 records to just one account.*

product. A solicitation cycle (the time it takes to solicit orders from each of the rep's accounts) is typically three weeks. Distributors send out monthly or semi-monthly books of one-sheets with all the new release information and order forms. Reps also visit the largest accounts in person during this cycle. They visit some but not all of the smaller accounts during the solicitation cycle, but will telephone even the small accounts regularly with information about new releases and sales breakthroughs.

**Credit cycle :**The distributor's ability to set up credit and collect payment for product makes him invaluable to both the label and the stores. He extends credit and accepts returns from stores. If a store doesn't pay its bill in 90 days, the distributor may refuse to ship it more records.

For a record retailer, the usual terms for purchasing records from a distributor are **net 90 days**, which means the record store has 90 days to pay for the product after receiving it. Cash flow is where major distributors have the advantage over you or anyone else selling to the chains or one-stops over other middlemen: they can afford to wait 90 days to get paid. This is also why chain stores or mass merchant accounts won't buy direct from record companies— they can get better terms (longer time to pay) through distributors.

**Sale pricing:** A sale price is a SRLP that is temporarily discounted. It may be a storewide retail program (such as Black Music Month sale, when selected black artists may be discounted by 10 percent or so), or it may be a discount paid for by the distributor or record label on a specific album (See **Co-op Advertising** and **Price and Position** later in this chapter).

**Special pricing:**  Older recordings—usually three years or older (sometimes called **catalog**)—often carry reduced or midline prices. Stores and consumers pay less for the recordings and artists receive less in

# How records go from major record companies to consumers

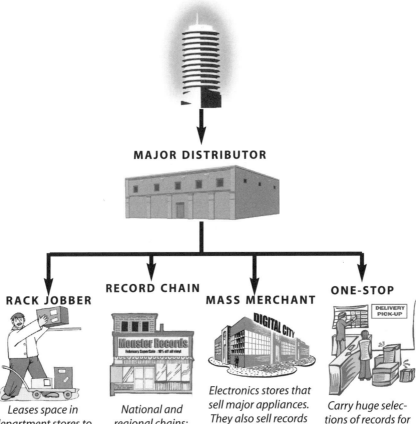

**MAJOR RECORD COMPANY**

**MAJOR DISTRIBUTOR**

**RACK JOBBER**

**RECORD CHAIN**

**MASS MERCHANT**

**ONE-STOP**

*Leases space in department stores to operate record departments. Racks include Handleman Company and Anderson's, who sell to accounts such as Kmart, Best Buy, and Wal-Mart*

*National and regional chains: Sam Goody, Virgin, Tower, Wherehouse, etc.*

*Electronics stores that sell major appliances. They also sell records just above cost to increase floor traffic for all departments: Best Buy, Circuit City*

*Carry huge selections of records for accounts that don't buy enough to purchase in bulk from major distributors*

**BOOKSTORES THAT SELL MUSIC**

**ONLINE MUSIC RETAILERS**

**"INDIE" RECORD STORES**

*Barnes & Noble, Borders, etc.*

*Amazon.com, CDNow.Com, etc.*

*Your neighborhood record store*

royalties. Special pricing is also found on many compilation albums, such as "Best Of" albums and theme albums (Greatest Love Songs, etc.) that include tracks by various artists on the same label.

## The Record Distribution Chain

**Major distributors** are usually owned and operated by conglomerates that also own record labels. Major distributors are primarily in the business of distributing the product (albums, singles, CDs, cassettes) manufactured by the parent conglomerates owned record labels and affiliates, including joint ventures and artist-owned labels. It is usually very difficult to get a major distributor to distribute product not affiliated with one of the conglomerate-owned record labels.

**Mass merchants** are the biggest retailers of music —not record stores, as you might think. A mass merchant is a large chain, such as Best Buy and Target, that doesn't specialize in music, but sells records at the lowest possible prices in its record departments to bring young buyers into the store (who may also purchase big-ticket electronics or sporting goods or clothing). Mass merchants also make money from the advertising they sell to record companies and distributors (**Co-op advertising**), which means that the album cover mini you see in the newspaper is paid for by the label or distributor, not by the store. Mass merchants' record departments are usually limited to the top 40 best sellers. They only carry between 1,500-5,500 different titles, compared to a large record store, which may carry 50,000 titles.

**Rack jobbers** are like major distributors that specialize in selling records through mass merchants. The differences between a rack jobber and a major distributor are:
1. A rack jobber leases space from mass merchants
2. Operates the store's music department in that space, making sure chart toppers are in stock. This

# How records go from "indie" record companies to consumers

### "INDIE" (INDEPENDENT RECORD COMPANY)

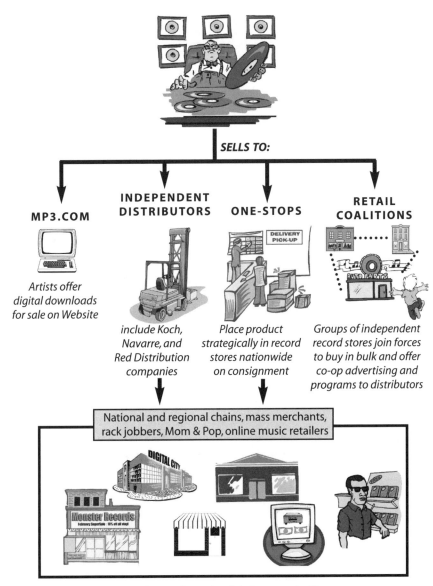

**SELLS TO:**

**MP3.COM**

**INDEPENDENT DISTRIBUTORS**

**ONE-STOPS**

**RETAIL COALITIONS**

*Artists offer digital downloads for sale on Website*

*include Koch, Navarre, and Red Distribution companies*

*Place product strategically in record stores nationwide on consignment*

*Groups of independent record stores join forces to buy in bulk and offer co-op advertising and programs to distributors*

National and regional chains, mass merchants, rack jobbers, Mom & Pop, online music retailers

*Records from independent labels are stocked by independent distributors and one-stops, who sell them to many kinds of stores*

frees the store buyers from the headache of ordering the right product in the right area at the right time.

3. Rack jobbers purchase product music directly from the distributors and put "racks" of current hits from all labels in stores alongside other merchandise that is actually controlled by the store.

One of the largest rack jobbers is Handleman, whose 3,000 employees manage over 5,000 stores around the world. Their accounts include Wal-Mart, Best Buy, and Kmart stores.

**Record chains** usually have separate buyers for each genre (type) of music. Each buyer targets different stores in the chain for different quantities of releases, according to the store's profile (the customers it brings in). This is the reason for classifying new acts according to genre. It doesn't necessarily mean that the artist only records a certain kind of music. It means that a store that specializes in R&B may get a standard allocation of records classified as R&B.

**One stops** (subdistributors) are outlets where small record stores buy their records. Since small stores don't have the budget or demand to buy huge quantities of any one title, they can go to a one-stop and buy just a few copies. The one-stop helps small stores by setting them up with "90 days to pay" credit terms. By the time payment is due, the record store has either sold enough records to pay for them, or returns the records that didn't sell and uses that money to buy other records.

## Independent Distribution

Back in the day, **independent distributors** distributed records for all major record labels—that is, until the labels set up their own distribution companies. Nowadays, independent distributors distribute records from **independent record labels** (those not distributed by the four big conglomerates). As the

# How independent production companies get their product into stores

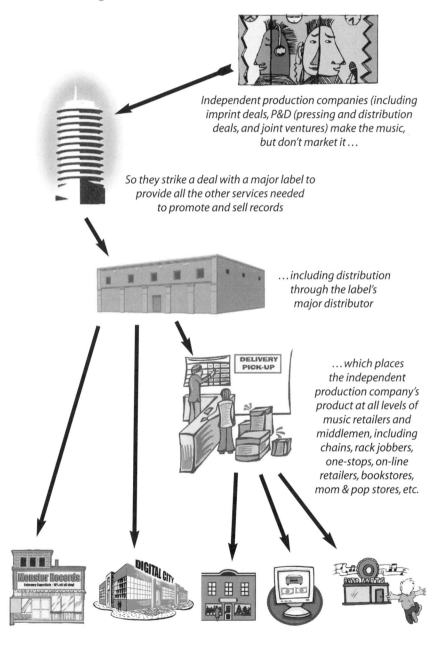

Independent production companies (including imprint deals, P&D (pressing and distribution deals, and joint ventures) make the music, but don't market it ...

So they strike a deal with a major label to provide all the other services needed to promote and sell records

... including distribution through the label's major distributor

... which places the independent production company's product at all levels of music retailers and middlemen, including chains, rack jobbers, one-stops, on-line retailers, bookstores, mom & pop stores, etc.

number of major conglomerates shrank over the past decade (there used to be six majors, now only four), "indie" distributors have made a resurgence. Indies specialize in "niche" music, such as Rap, Gospel, and Crunk music (southern Hip-hop), and are considered experts in their fields. They are occasionally purchased by major distributors looking to increase the distribution of their own niche market records.

*Independent retailers* ("Indies" or "Mom and Pop" retailers) are local record stores that are not owned by a parent company and usually buy product from a one-stop (subdistributor) that provides them with a line of credit. Indies may join retail coalitions so they can compete with chains in some areas, such as sale pricing, co-op advertising, and other promotions.

*Retail coalitions*—a relatively new concept— are groups of small Mom & Pop record stores that pool their buying power so they can buy in large quantities to get volume discounts, offer sales programs, get co-op advertising, and earn free goods.

Retail coalitions may place retail ads in the distributor's monthly mailer, or install a listening booth in a coalition member's establishment.

With the explosion of mass retail merchants (Target, Best Buy, etc.) in the music marketplace and the incentives distributors offer them, it's tough for small stores to stay competitive. Because independent stores tend to purchase product in small quantities, they rarely receive co-op advertising dollars or price & position programs from record labels, or purchase enough product to get deep discounts and free goods. Recently, however, independent stores have formed coalitions in order to leverage their buying power as a group and get some of the big guys' perks. Independent retail coalitions have proven fertile ground for breaking new and independent artists. Usually owned and operated by true–blue music fans, small specialty stores have direct access to consumers and can hand-sell records to their customers. Labels are learning how to use retail coalitions to start a product buzz.

### THE PREORDER PROCESS: Getting new records into stores at the same time from coast to coast

**Preorders** are the orders the distributors request from retailers prior to releasing a new record. The purpose is to ship all the new product at once so it is in stores and available to consumers by the **street date**. This is accomplished by sending **sales solicitations** (**one-sheets**) to all retail accounts.

A **one-sheet** contains all the information a retailer or wholesaler (one-stop, etc.) needs in order to determine how much to purchase on a new release. It includes the artist's name, title, selection number (catalog number), and genre (type of music). It also includes artist information, sales history, key selling points, the label's marketing plans, P.O.P. available, the record's bar code, and an order form that can be faxed or called in. One-sheets are usually sent to the distributors' accounts (stores, one-stops, etc.) 8–12 weeks prior to the street date.

**Street date** is the calendar date by which time product is scheduled to be in retail stores and available to consumers. Most major distributors have one or two street dates most months—usually Tuesdays. Going "off cycle"—that is, shipping a record between scheduled street dates—is more expensive and a poor excuse to neglect all the preparation for marketing the record properly.

## Press and Distribute Deal

In a **press and distribute** deal, a small or independent record label joins forces with a larger or more established record label that agrees to manufacture (press) and distribute (get the product into the stores). For this service, the distributing label receives

### Why is the business of selling records at Kmart or Best Buy so different from that of record stores?

*To stay in business and sell at the lowest prices, mass merchants must squeeze every drop of profit from every square foot of the store space. Stores constantly figure what each department sells per square foot and decide to add or subtract space from every area.*

*Bottom line: there is great pressure to sell the most merchandise in the smallest space. That's why the record departments are often small and carry only proven hits and best-sellers.*

# How to make a one-sheet

**ONE-SHEETS *MUST* INCLUDE:**

- **Artist name**
- **Album title and photo (mini)**
- **Selection (catalog) number**
- **Street date**
- **Distributor contact**
- **Genre (type of music)**
- **Price or price code**

**ONE-SHEETS *SHOULD* INCLUDE:**

- **Bar code (UPC)**
- **Box lots:** How many units ship in a box
- **Artist bio:** A paragraph of background information, description of musical style, names of previous albums and hit songs, industry awards, some quotes from the artist
- **Album description:** Interesting info about this release—where or when it was recorded, overall lyrical themes, famous songwriters, guest artists, producers, engineers, or recording facilities used
- **Marketing info:** Artist's hometown and regions of strongest fan support, radio stations that have played artist's music
- **Sales History:** SoundScan information or sales figures on previous releases, especially in hottest areas

## Artist Name
*Album title*

Seen and heard by tens of thousands in 2005 Artist Name presents the follow-up to his deb

**HE HAS BEEN DESCRIBED AS ...**

the next big thing in the world of pop/jazz fusion hybrids, Artist Name pulls together some of the biggest soloists in the field on his new album.

The artist has shared the stage with an "A" list of pop and R&B talent, including Janine Adams, Vickie Williams, Mary Rowley, Danny Hawkins, Timmy Teens, and Ricky Durante.

*LP title* —his new, self-produced album—also features urban/hip-hop tracks and live performances. combines fresh sounds, urban beats, and an eclectic selection of songs in his musical feast.

Last year he performed at the International Pop Celebration in Miami. The awesome show was seen by hundreds of radio announcers and DJs from across the country. Recently, the group made their national television debut on the *Entertainment Today Show* with rave reviews.

**BIO**

A classically-trained pianist, the artist began playing in his school at 4. At 17 he took the Gold Medal in Music Composition at the regional Sonata competition—winning with a musical score for a 30-piece orchestra. He developed into a gifted singer, songwriter, producer, composer, and video director, and also plays organ, drums, keyboards, and guitar. The artist opened for Harry Williams Love Fest with a piano instrumental, and has also appeared on ABC-TV, as the lead voice of orchestral group Name.

**TOUR**
- Jan 20: Cellar Door, Washington, DC
- Jan. 21 Quiet Side, Landover, MD
- Jan. 24: Northern Virginia Community College
- Jan. 28: Jazz Power Convention, Philadelphia
- Jan. 29: City Auditorium, Lancaster, PA
- Feb. 2: Gaslight Club, New Orleans, LA
- More dates booked—go to www.golightly.com

**GENRES:** R&B, Pop, Jazz

| ARTIST, Title | CD WM-7020-2 Box Lot-30 pcs | $16.99 Qty: |

# *that really sells your product*

Album Cover

RKETING & PROMOTION

.O.P.
Album flats
Shelf Talkers

PRE-STREET PROMOTIONS
♦ **Convention Promotions**
Pop Celebration National Convention in
Miami, Florida: Board of Directors
Meeting, March 2002. Announcements,
advertising and advance copies of the
CD to Music Directors, Program
Directors, Radio and delegates.
♦ Aggressive Music Director and DJ
Pre-Sales Promotion campaign

NATIONAL RADIO ROLLOUT
Heavy concentration at radio starting in
the Santa Margarita area and saturating the
entire market. Radio promotions to 1200+
pop and R&B radio announcers.

SPECIAL PROMOTIONS
The project will be featured within the 336
chapter, 30,000-member strong Miami Pop
Celebration Committee.

CUSTOMER ADVERTISING
BUYS

**Distributed by**
(Distributor contact info)

$11.99
Qty:

© 2005

• **Track listing:** Song-by-song list of the artist and titles. If some tracks were previously released or were a chart success, give the specifics.

• **Single or Focus Track:** List the singles that will be worked at radio, brief description of the track (upbeat? ballad? instrumental? Smokin' lead guitar?) List what music formats will be serviced and when. If there are no radio singles, suggest a few focus tracks for buyers to hear.

• **Merchandising tools:** Will POP (point-of-purchase) or display materials such as flats, posters, or postcards be created? Bin cards, cassette shelf-talkers, keychains for radio giveaways? In-store samplers? Don't forget to list your one-sheet.

• **Video:** List if and when a video be available for any tracks. Will it be serviced to press or specialty programs?

• **Tour dates:** List upcoming dates or regions where the artist will perform (e.g. "West Coast tour this summer") in support of the release. List markets where the artist has built a following through previous touring.

• **Press:** Include quotes from feature articles, reviews of the release or live performances.

• **Non-Traditional marketing:** Name marketing companies hired to work the record. Mention products the artist is affiliated with (e.g. instrument or equipment sponsors), or corporate tie-ins that will be pursued.

• **Internet information:** Include artist or label Website information, fan sites, bulletin boards, and discussion groups.

a fee or royalty, usually between 18 and 20 percent of the wholesale price. The remaining profit goes to the smaller label. Out of the smaller label's profit must come the expense of manufacturing and any other expenses directly related to selling the album, such as marketing and promotions, mechanical license, artist royalties, employee salaries, office overhead, etc.

A press and distribute deal seems enticing because the smaller label retains its autonomy and receives some 80 percent of the revenue from record sales, although the small label must pay for the costs of manufacturing and distribution. Nonetheless, press and distribute deals are becoming increasingly rarer for the following reasons.

1. Most major record labels are now owned and operated by large profit driven corporations that must report to their shareholders, so the major labels pass on these deals in favor of deals that give them a larger percentage of the profits.

2. The smaller record label rarely has theresources to fund a really good marketing and promotional campaign. Smaller labels generally need to acquire the services of the major label and usually lean on the label's marketing and promotion departments. In return, the major label must charge extra fees for extending their services. At the same time, the independent record label is competing against the major label for airplay, retail space, and special programs, etc. If there's only one spot available at a radio station for airplay and the major label is working their product as well, guess who gets the slot?

3. Because the smaller label is paying a fee for distribution, it can end up losing money because the distributing or major label receives a fee

regardless if the records are returned or not. If the smaller label gets too many returns it will soon be out of business.

The press and distribute deals works best particularly when the distributed label controls a niche market share, understands its specific market, and has as an artist that is well-known within the genre, such as Reggae music, Rap or Gospel.

If the independent label is self-sufficient and contains its own marketing and promotion departments, and if all the different elements are in place already, the label doesn't really need a press and distribute deal. It should sign directly with a distributor, like some of the early rap labels and most classical labels have done.

## More Distribution Speak ...

**Reserve** is a percentage—usually 30 percent—of money owed to record labels by distributors that is withheld to cover the cost of shipping returns back from the stores (returns are records the stores were unable to sell and are returned to the distributor for full credit). The distributor pays the cost of shipping records to stores, but the label pays the cost of shipping back returned product. The distributor can hold onto that 30 percent reserve for six months to cover returns. The reason for reserves is that records, unlike many other types of products, are 100 percent returnable and can be unpredictable. The record company also withholds reserves from artists' royalties for up to six to twelve months. Reserves candrastically reduce cash flow, but it is a standard industry practice.

**Cross-collateralization** is a standard accounting procedure that most distributors require in their contracts with labels. It means that if a label has two records out—one is losing money and the other is making money—the distributor has the right to take losses from one record out of revenues from

### So, you think you have a record label...

*Think again ... without distribution, a record label is a glorified production company. Record labels' strengths lie in their abilities to take a record from concept to consumer. But until you secure regional or national distribution, you are not a fully functional record label.*

the profitable record.

For example: Your label puts out records "A" and "B." "A" is successful, but "B" is not—stores want to return it as fast as possible. But when the return rate is more than 30 percent of the money the distributor owes the record company, the distributor starts to lose money (remember, he only gets to withhold 30 percent of the money he owes the distributor). Around this time, the distributor will start to limit the amount of returns. Stores have 90 days to pay the distributor for the records, and want to return the nonsellers before they have to pay for them.

**Returns** are records that do not sell and are returned from the stores back to the distributor for credit. Virtually all records sold to stores in the United States carry a 100 percent return privilege. If a retailer orders more than he can sell, he simply ships the product back to the distributor for full credit (refund) or exchange for other titles. Record distributors offer this policy to retailers to ensure there's plenty of product in the market when an album hits the streets. Once a record is a hit, of course, everyone wants to stock it. But until then, retailers may not be willing to sink their limited cash or credit into a product by an unproven act. Since stores have 60 to 90 days to pay for product, the goal is to return the records that don't sell before the bill arrives so they never have to pay for product that doesn't sell.

**Catalog** is the backbone of the industry. The catalog is the master recordings that the label owns. It's one thing to put out new artists and break records, but the real "meat" of the business is the catalog, which provides a constant stream of income year after year with little or no additional cost to the label. The legendary Motown Records, for instance, owns master recordings by such artists as Marvin Gaye, Stevie Wonder, the Jackson 5, and the Supremes. These titles can be repackaged into all sorts of compilations and greatest hits packages and sold for generations to come. Every ten years a new generation discovers Bob Marley and the Eagles and purchases these Evergreen titles. This is why ownership of master recordings is vital to the record label: it provides the funds to break new artists.

**Disintermediation** is a fancy buzz word that means cutting out the middleman so consumers can buy directly from the creators of the product. An example is digital downloadable formats, which eliminate the need for printing, pressing, and warehouses—as well as the need for record stores, wholesalers, one-stops, retail stores, and packaging. This seems to be where the record business is heading. Already, consumers can download music and graphics and print and assemble CD packages.

The record company of the future may be more of an online service that provides marketing and promotion for a fee to the artist. The challenge is making the consumer aware of new music and discovering new ways to break records in the future. There's a record company now that markets its artists by attaching a mini-CD to the lids of soda containers sold at movie theaters.

**Bar code (UPC code)** consists of a pattern and number that is printed on almost every product sold in the United States. In the record business, bar codes are usually printed on the back covers of the CDs and cassettes in such a way that they can be read by a bar code scanner. The bar code identifies the manufacturer, configuration, and selection number (catalog number). Bar code numbers are assigned by the Universal Code Council. Bar codes revolutionized many things, including inventory control for many industries, and even the *Billboard* charts, which tally bar codes scanned at stores around the country.

### Another kind of catalog

*In 1919—only two decades after the first recordings were made—Victor Records published a catalog listing works by classical composers and any recorded performances of those works.*

6 -47867-7026-2 5

*first series of 5 digits indicates record label*

*4-digit catalog number*

*configuration (2= CD)*

***Co-op advertising*** (cooperative advertising) is a method of advertising or promoting records where the retailer and record label share in the expense. For example, you may see a group of albums advertised with a retailer's logo or tag ("Available at Target"). Both parties may split the cost, or the distributor may provide a discount on product sold to the retailer, or the label may agree to pay for the ad if the retailer agrees to buy a specific amount of product.

***P.O.P.*** (point- of-purchase materials) promote records or artists and are placed in the view of the consumer at stores. P.O.P. includes posters, flats (12" x 12" color prints of album cover), shelf-talkers, and countertop displays that hold product (holding 30 CDs, for example), and artist cutouts/standups. Such materials are usually available to stores through distributors' sales reps. Record labels send P.O.P along with the product ordered, and the distributor stores it and provides it to specific accounts.  Usually the store can indicate an order for P.O.P. on their product order form. Stores may be able to buy it at cost, or the distributor may agree to give a specific amount of P.O.P.  at no-charge, based on the value of an order.

***Online music retailers*** take orders online through their Websites, and then ship physical CDs via mail. You can sell product by linking to online music stores that will sell, ship, and collect payment for physical product, such as www.CDBaby.com, the top independent store on the Web. They will sell your product directly, assist in manufacturing, and send you a check.

Established sites such as Amazon.com or CDnow can help sell product for the independent record label. They provide one of the best forms of distribution outside of conventional stores and can build a good fanbase on the Web.

**Record clubs** are usually joint ventures owned by several distributors that sell records through mail order, such as Columbia House. Record clubs are another way for records to reach consumers. The agreement between the record club and member usually requires the member to purchase a certain number of records within a year. In exchange, the member gets a number of free records. Record clubs, in turn, require labels to give them a certain amount of free records, which become the free records you choose when you join a club. In most cases, record clubs don't purchase records from the labels, but license the right to manufacture records for their club members. Out of that product they have the right to manufacture a certain amount as free goods. Occasionally clubs will buy finished goods instead of manufacturing their own.

**Price and position** are two ways stores can greatly increase sales. Offering a sale price on a CD and putting it in a special display in the front of the store are two of the most attractive attention-getters to browsing buyers. The sale price and prime position are also referred to as buy-ins because the label must pay for these programs either by discounting the price of records ordered, or by providing a certain percentage of free records with every record sold.

The retailer charges labels for such programs, which include featuring product at listening stations, in newspaper ads, in window displays, and "artist of the week" programs (and you thought stores did all that stuff for free!). Labels usually figure these prices into the marketing and promotional budgets. The cost is normally based on giving somewhere between $1 and $1.50 per unit purchased to the purchasing store for buy-in programs. If a dealer buys 8,000 records, for example, he knows in advance he'll receive between $8,000 and $12,000 for advertising buy-ins.

Occasionally a retailer assigns a sale price with no conditions, such as during Black Music Month, when

all R&B titles may be discounted. Distributors often run price and position programs in the first three to six weeks of an album's release in order to get the product charted quickly and create a buzz early on.

***Solicitation date/period*** begins when a distributor starts soliciting his accounts for preorders on new product, usually 8–12 weeks before the album's street date. The solicitation period is how long it takes the distributor to round up orders from all his accounts, usually about three weeks.

## Other Ways Records are Sold

### How do you sell music on the Internet?
Online music sales via the Internet are revolutionizing the way music is sold. Making music available to consumers via the Internet makes it possible for the novice or independent musician or artist to circulate his or her album to the masses. ***The most important tool in selling music over the Internet is a professional Website.*** For an independent, this becomes the hub of all activity, so make sure it's of the highest possible quality. Check out other record company or artist Websites for content ideas, and constantly update your Website with new information. Research shows that people who revisit a Website and see that nothing has changed are unlikely to return. Update your tour schedules and live performances. Include photos and an online press kit. Also, your Website should contain an e-mail address where your fans and customers can send you messages. Make audio downloadable samples available for prospective customers to preview. It's crucial to constantly update your content to keep your fans interested and returning to your site.

There are several methods for selling product through your Website. You can set it up as an e-commerce site where you accept credit card payments for record sales shipped directly to consumers. Or you can use an Internet fulfillment service that you link to your

Website and who will accept the payment and ship the product to consumers for you. You can also list your product at online retailer Websites like Amazon.com, which sells music and has a link from your Website to theirs so they can go directly to your product page on the Amazon's Website. In many cases the consumer is more comfortable making a purchase with a larger well-known retailer such as Amazon. There are some fee-based Websites that specialize in selling records, and you can have your own web pages and bio information listed.

## *Online CD Retailers*

### *CD Baby*
***www.cdbaby.com***
CD Baby is the largest online record store that sells CDs by independent record labels and artist/musicians. They only sell CDs that come directly from the independent record label's musicians or artists. They do not deal with distributors or middlemen of any kind. Independent labels send the CDs directly to them. CD Baby warehouses them, sells them to the consumers, and pays the artist or independent record label directly on a weekly basis. The independent label artist and musicians can make $6–$12 per CD.

### *CD Street*
***www.cdstreet.com***
CD Street is an online store that actually reports to Soundscan and allows the artist to accept credit card payments at gigs. Check out their Website.

***Digital Distribution*** is a relatively new technology that is still developing. It allows consumers to download music from legal, royalty-paying online services, onto computers and portable players, such as the Apple iPod. Prices per track range from 49¢ to $1.14. The download provider pays the copyright owners (songwriters and label) for each song sold. This new concept will eventually change how we buy music. But given widespread practice of illegal filesharing,

### *Websites are the cornerstones...*

*of all promotion, marketing, and distribution efforts for independent artists who plan to sell their own recordings.* The possibilities are endless. A Website allows:

- *The world to find and listen to your music.*

- *You to sell downloads of your music and artwork and anything else digital.*

- *You to flash your personality to the world—start a buzz.*

- *You to advertise yourself to a billion Internet users*

- *You to describe your goals and find people to help you accomplish them.*

it is difficult for labels and online distributors to convince people to pay for music they've been getting for free.

Apple, one of the first to forge deals with all five major conglomerates, operates the iTunes store at www.apple.com. They claim to have sold more than 500 million songs and offer 1.5 million selections. Other download services include Buymusic.com and liquid.com.

Small record labels can set up payments for downloads by setting up a merchant account or using a service that handles credit card transactions, such as PayPal, which ensures payment for every download.

Eventually, almost all music sales will be digital downloads. Record companies will become marketing and promotion companies.

**Mail order** is also an effective way of selling records. It eliminates the wholesaler and retailer, increasing profit margins. Retailers usually advertise through TV or print ads. Mail order has proven successful with the Time Life series. Mail order is also a way you can sell records on your own Website.

# Product Development Schedule

***88 days before release date***: Street date is determined by the record label and then given to the distributor, along with all information pertaining to release.

***67 days before release date:*** One- sheets containing all pertinent information for the release are delivered to distributors to solicit pre-orders from retail accounts.

***53 days before release date:*** Promotion material is delivered to sales reps and is sent out to various retail and radio outlets and media outlets.

***25 days before release date***: The finished, manufactured product is delivered to the distributors' warehouses from the manufacturing plant to prepare for shipment to retail accounts, in order to be in stores by the street date.

## Six suggestions to establish a solid presence on the Internet

1. *Set up an e-mail account*
2. *Design a professional Website*
3. *List your Website with all the search engines*
4. *Submit your music to Internet radio stations*
5. *Provide audio samples of your music on your Website*
6. *Promote your Website during performances and interviews*

# 2.

# Creating the Product

The recording process has advanced with the rise of digital technology. Twenty years ago, an album might cost between $100,000 and $500,000 to record, using analog technology in a 24-track studio with a sound engineer. Today, using digital technology (a tapeless format), your average home computer and a few basic accessories enable you to record and mix an entire album in your home for a fraction of the cost. With the invention of the digital sequencer, it's possible for one person to play and layer all the different instruments. With the invention of the Akai MPC-60 and the Emu SP 1200 drum machines, one self-contained producer can make an entire album for between $15,000 and $20,000. What took hundreds of people to do 20 years ago can now be handled by one person.

One positive result of digital recording was Rap music—one of the first big users of digital technology in the early '80s. Rap music costs a fraction of what other genres cost to record, and so it became very attractive to record labels. Another consequence of digital recording is that record companies have reduced recording budgets.

## Recording Budget

The recording budget is the total amount allocated by the label to record a song or an entire album. The amount is determined by:
- Previous sales history
- Belief factor—how much the label believes the artist will become a popular seller
- The kind of consumer the act will appeal to

## What is A&R?

A&R—"Artist and Repertoire"—is the department that finds new talent and selects songs for artists to record. Over the years, A&R has expanded its territory and now has the power to:

**1** **Sign new talent.**

**2** **Act as the all-round go-to staff** for artists, making sure they get to the studio/photo shoot/wherever they're needed.

**3** **Introduce artists** to producers.

**4** **Help define a look and style** —or help select the right stylist—a critical decision now that music videos are so influential. Artists may be seen on TV or in print before they are heard. Video images will be seen by more people on television than the music alone can reach.

**5** **Guide the artist in a musical direction.**

## How do you record an album with P.O.s?

*Let's say a producer hires a background vocalist for $1,500. The producer sends her a purchase order (P.O.) signed by the record company, which promises to pay her after she provides her services. A copy of the P.O. is also sent to the A&R administration department, which issues payments to musicians, singers, equipment rentals, etc.*

*After the musician performs, she sends an invoice for $1,500— with the P.O. number written on it—to the A&R administration department. If the amount on her bill matches the P.O. they have on file, the invoice is paid without further delay.*

• Genre (type of music) - The budget is usually stated in the recording agreement, often on a step-up or inclining basis, which means the first album receives the minimum amount. A typical album budget for a new artist on a major label ranges from $125,000-$300,000. If the contract provides for future recordings, budgets can range up to millions of dollars if the initial records are successful.

Usually each department (R&B, Pop, Jazz, Classical, etc.) receives a set portion of the label's total operating budget for the year based on what the company expects each department to sell. For instance, the operating budget of the jazz department is probably less than the budget for the pop department.

Out of this fund, the A&R department must sign the artist, record the album, hire producers, and pay advances. Once the artist is signed and budgets and cash advances are determined, the budget is passed on to the legal, A&R administration, and accounting departments. After selecting the producer, A&R makes the producer fully responsible for delivering records on budget by signing an agreement with him.

Producers manage their budgets by two methods:

*1. Purchase order* The producer is given a percentage of the budget up front, as an advance payment against future royalties. He issues numbered purchase orders to promise payment (from the record label) for all production costs. He is still responsible for delivering product within the budget, including hiring studios, musicians, singers, equipment, and delivering finished product.

The purchase order system works best for large companies that musicians and other suppliers know will pay on time. It is more difficult for smaller labels and independent production companies. Musicians, rental companies, etc., may require payment up front or in cash on the day of the session (COD). Whatever portion of the budget that is not spent stays in the overall recording fund and reduces the amount that is recouped from the artist before royalties are paid.

**2. All-In budget** After the producer is hired and the budget is determined, the record company releases the entire budget to the producer, usually in two or three lump sum payments. Whatever is left over after the completed master is accepted by the label belongs to the producer or production company.

With the rise of superstar producers in recent years and new technology for the home studio, the all-in budget has become increasingly popular. The average producer has the facilities and equipment to make a start-to-finish product without spending much additional money.

The all-in budget allows the producer (usually an experienced, in-demand producer whom the label trusts) to make more money by spending less than the budget allows. In some cases, a superstar producer can demand as much as $250,000 for a song. But because he owns and operates his own recording studio, he can record all the instruments, sing the background vocals, and deliver the record for less than $30,000. Either way—via all-in budget or purchase order—the total cash outlay for the recording process must be fully recouped before the producer receives any future royalties.

### *Master purchase (Selling out)*
When an artist, producer, or independent record label completes an entire recording project without outside financing (such as a recording budget provided by a major label), and then sells the finished master recording to a label, the transaction is called a master purchase. The producer and artist receive a lump sum from the sale and the same royalties as if they'd received a recording budget from the

### *How do you record an album with an "all-in" budget?*

*If a budget for a song is $30,000, the producer may receive $15,000 when he begins to record it, and $15,000 when he turns in the finished track. Whatever portion of the budget is not spent belongs to the producer. So if the track only cost the producer $25,000, he keeps the extra $5,000.*

**MONEY TALKS**

label. In other words, the ownership of the master is transferred to the label in exchange for cash and a percentage of profits.

Master purchases are common for smaller, independent companies whose talent is creating product, but who are unable to meet the demands or costs of marketing or breaking an act. So the small company sells a finished product to a larger company that can provide the promotion and marketing required to turn records into hits.

## People Who Create the Sound

### What the producer does

The producer is responsible for delivering a finished master recording to the record company. He makes creative contributions to a recording's sound and feel, based on his choices of sound engineers, musicians, equipment, microphones, and song selection. Once the company accepts the recording, it pays the producer the balance of his fee.

Besides determining the creative direction of the record, the producer is responsible for managing the budget, whether for one song or an entire album. He agrees to deliver the completed master recording within the budget he receives from his client (the record company) by a certain date. Out of the budget, he pays for studio time, hires musicians and background singers, rents equipment, etc. In order to receive full or final payment, the producer delivers a complete two-track (stereo) recording to the record company, ready to be mastered.

The producer usually receives a portion of his recording budget as an advance payment against his future royalties. His fees, including an advance payment, must be paid back to the record company ("recouped") before he starts receiving royalties. The producer's royalty is usually between 3 percent and 6 percent of the record's retail earnings. So if a record has a list price of $16.98, the producers' total share would be about 85¢ per record sold.

If one person produces all the songs on the album, he receives the entire producer's royalty. If some songs are produced by other producers, each producer's share of royalties is prorated. In other words, producers are paid in proportion to how many songs they produce on an album.

Frequently the producer's hit-making ability is more powerful than the artist's. Today the record business is basically a producer-driven business. There are many producers who have a trademark or signature sound—such as Jam and Lewis and Babyface—and whose names are more recognizable than the artists they record.

Some signature sounds are so recognizable that consumers will buy their records regardless of the recording artist. For these reasons, record companies try to make deals with artists associated with signature-sound producers.

### Executive producer

An executive producer usually performs some special function for the project. She may be the person who puts up money to record the album or a record company employee that helps guide the project.

The executive producer's role tends to be administrative or financial, not creative. She may be responsible for allocating the budget to the producer, or hiring or assisting the producer, or parceling out funds for the entire project.

On a project with multiple producers, the executive

## What is creative control?

*As assigned in a recording contract, creative control is the right to determine the creative direction of a production. It can be crucial in an industry where companies tend to use cookie-cutter formulas to emulate success rather than explore new ground. Hits by emulation do have a place because there are certain formulas for making hits. But the biggest new successes are those that break through with something new. Formulas can hinder an artist's creative expression, especially if the artist is unique— such as a Nora Jones or Jill Scott—and doesn't fit neatly into a particular genre or style.*

producer is usually an employee of the record company responsible for hiring the producers and determining their budgets. It's not unusual for an executive producer to receive a royalty for her services.

### Coproducer

Similar to a producer, the coproducer makes fewer contributions and final decisions, and always in conjunction with the producer. Coproducers usually receive a small royalty.

### Recording engineers

Two types of engineers are used in the recording process:

- A **tracking engineer** is responsible for recording sessions of tracks, which are the individual sounds (such as vocal sessions or instruments). The tracking engineer can help determine the sound through his various recording techniques, such as microphone placements, equipment, or different "tricks."

- A **mix engineer** specializes only in mixing together those individual tracks. His skills can greatly enhance a project and he may have a trademark sound. He usually has his own equipment, which is used exclusively to maintain sound quality and consistency. High-profile mix engineers usually have working relationships with certain producers. In some cases the mix engineer's sound is such a significant contribution that he may receive percentage points from the record's sales in addition to a healthy fee somewhere between $2,000 to $6,000 per mix. Some mix engineers even have their own managers.

# Musicians & Performers

### Featured or Guest artist

When a recording artist signed to one record company performs on an album owned by another company, it is considered to be a featured or guest artist performance. This happens when, for example, an instrumentalist signed to an exclusive recording contract is invited to perform on an album being released by a singer on another label. Or, in modern times, a well-known Hip-hop DJ may include guest appearances from well-known Rap stars on his album.

Typically, the featured or guest artist receives an artist royalty for the song on which he's featured. The artist royalty is pro rata, which means the featured or guest artist receives one-tenth (one track's worth) of the total album artist royalty. In most cases, the featured or guest artist also would like to receive an advance on future royalties. The advance can range from $2,500 to $50,000+—depending solely on the marketability of the featured artist.

In the event that the featured or guest artist is under a recording agreement of his own, it's necessary to obtain a release from the record company. The guest artist's record company can also demand a portion of the royalties in addition to an "**appears courtesy of**" credit.

### Session musician

A session musician is a musician for hire who interprets a song on her instrument, thereby making a musical contribution to the project. Musicians are generally paid by union scale guidelines, which are

## How does being a "guest artist" work?

*Let's say recording artist "A," signed to Acorn Records, invites guest artist "B" to perform a sax solo on his album. "A" agrees to split his royalty for the track with "B"—although if "B" were invited to sing the song, "A" would probably give up his entire royalty for the track. So if "A" gets a 10% royalty rate, on a $16.98 record, that would amount to $1.69 (for the whole album) divided by the number of tracks (let's say 10), or 16.9¢ per CD sold. "B" will want an advance on future royalties the song is likely to earn—usually between $2,500 and $50,000. "B" obtains a release (i.e., permission) from his label, Badguy Records, for this particular project, and makes sure that "A" adds this credit to his album package: " 'B' appears courtesy of Badguy Records."*

based on a three-hour minimum and an overtime rate if the session lasts longer. The session musician is paid a one-time fee and receives no royalties, nor does she have creative rights to her contribution. A session musician who appears on many big-selling albums may qualify for a yearly bonus from the union.

Session musicians are considered the best musicians, professionals who devote their lives to becoming the best in their field. But because the recording business is turning into a home-studio recording business, producers now play most of the instrumental parts. With digital wizardry, less expertise is required because sequencers can play complex music as fast as needed and expert licks can be sampled. As a result, session musicians are finding less work in pop music and more in movie scores, soundtracks, commercials, underscoring, and "cue" music.

### Session leader

A session leader is the lead musician on a union session. He is responsible for making sure that union rules and procedures are followed, and acts as a liaison between contractor or producer and the musicians at the session. The session leader is responsible for filing accurate session reports and reporting the musicians tax information to the union. For these reasons, the session leader usually receives higher pay.

### Union sponsor

In order for a record company to pay musicians through the musicians union, the company must be registered as a Musician's Union sponsor. Once a sponsor, a label is required to follow all union rules or pay penalties. One of those rules is that *all* the label's sessions must consist of union musicians. Labels that don't follow union rules—which list nonunion musicians on the album covers, for example—are subject to fines.

### Production coordinator

The production coordinator is usually an employee of

the record company or is hired by the producer to make sure everything goes smoothly at a recording session. She is responsible for notifying musicians about the time and location of their sessions, confirming that studio time is booked, having food delivered by caterers, and seeing that the session leader fills out the proper union paperwork. The coordinator also makes sure that each person is properly credited for his contribution by collecting and compiling the names of the musicians and caterers and making sure they're spelled correctly. She sends the information to the label, which lists such *credits* on the album packaging.

## Packaging: The Visual Side of Music

### Art director
The art director is responsible for the visual image of the artist in print, on posters, and point-of-purchase displays.

### Graphic designer
Similar to the art director, a graphic designer may be a record company employee or a freelancer (independent designer) in charge of laying out credits (printed information on the album package) and images into a package design. More than ever, the visual image can make or break an artist because it's often the consumer's first impression of the artist.

### Stylist

The stylist is an image designer and tastemaker that has gained importance over past 20 years as the record business switched from a music-driven industry to an image-driven industry. Today, the visual image of the artist may be more powerful than the artistic ability.

The stylist helps the label, manager, and artist determine the image artist's visual image. The stylist assembles a distinctive look that includes clothing, hair style, accessories, and makeup. Versions of the stylization will be used for photo shoots, video shoots, and personal appearances.

### Artist development

The process of getting an artist ready for mass exposure is handled by a label's artist development department. The modern-day concept was introduced by Berry Gordy at Motown Records in the 1960s as a sort of boot camp for artists. Most major labels now have an artist development department where artists learn how to present themselves in public. Speech therapists may be hired; choreographers can smooth out dance moves; singing coaches will polish styles; and tutors can teach proper dining etiquette. This education ensures that an artist is polished and confident in public. Most artists will take part in mock TV and radio interview sessions where they learn to answer questions in an accurate and entertaining manner that will benefit—not harm—the artist. Stylists and photographers are brought in to create and maintain a consistent image throughout a campaign.

## The Tools that Shape Sound

### Pro mixing console

A professional mixing console is usually used in the process of mixing. Over 90 percent of *Billboard*'s No. 1 records are mixed on the popular English-built, solid

**PARENTAL ADVISORY EXPLICIT CONTENT**

### What's the point of a Parental Advisory?

*A Parental Advisory is a warning printed on a package to alert parents to product that may be inappropriate for younger audiences. Seen frequently on Hip-hop and Rock records, it is a voluntary measure of the major labels, particularly RIAA members, which are expected to comply. It is designed to protect children and to protect record labels from parental lawsuits.*

state logic mixing console, better known as SSL. Some newer hits are being mixed on virtual consoles, which are basically home computers that become mixing consoles after adding special software. Professional consoles can cost $1 million or more, and the virtual consoles (made up of hardware and software) can cost around $10,000 up to $100,000-plus.

### Pro Tools

Pro Tools is a software package for professional sound and digital audio editing, first created under the name Sound Tools by Digidesign, now a division of Avid. It is widely used in the post production, music, and radio industries, and serves as the de facto standard in some segments of those industries.

As one of the first programs to provide CD-quality (16-bit and 44.1 kHz) multitrack editing on a personal computer, Pro Tools quickly grew into a widely-used program in the sound recording field. It became popular in the early 1990s primarily because it offered an interface modeled after the analog hardware to which most producers were accustomed, in addition to digital technology such as plugins, effects, MIDI functionality, and advanced non-linear audio editing capabilities.

Pro Tools systems generally fall into three categories, depending on the user's needs and budget. *Pro Tools Free* was released as an entry-level application and is the only version of Pro Tools that does not require Digidesign hardware. It is limited to 8 audio tracks and runs on Windows 98 and Mac OS 9 only.

### Drum machine

A drum machine is a sequencer with a synthesizer component that is tailored to the MIDI note numbers specified for drums. The General MIDI specification reserves MIDI channel 10 for this purpose. They are specialized for the creation of rhythms by playing synthesized or sampled drum sounds in a predetermined order.

**Why are mixing consoles so expensive?**

*Converting audio (analog sound) to high-quality digital sound is a very tricky (i.e., costly) process. The software and hardware are less expensive if you buy consumer versions (made by Digidesign, for example). Each brand has a distinct sound. Inexpensive components can drastically affect sound quality, especially at high volume. Most hits are mixed on high-end consoles that take in a lot of power through precisely designed transformers and resistors without distorting sound.*

The original drum machines were referred to as rhythm machines because they only played preprogrammed rhythms such as mambo, tango, etc. In1980 user-programmable drum machines appeared, allowing musicians to create any rhythm they wanted. The Roland TR-808 was one of the first and most popular of the programmable drum machines, and the sounds from that machine have become pop music clichés, heard on countless recordings. Early examples such as the TR-series used a method of synchronization called DIN-synch, or synch-24. Some of these machines also output analog voltages CV/Gate that could be used to synchronize or control analog synthesizers and other music equipment.

Drum machines are typically programmed by specifying which sixteenth notes of a bar a given drum will sound on. By stringing differently-programmed bars together, fills, breaks, rhythmic changes, and longer phrases can be created. Drum machine controls typically include Tempo, Start and Stop, volume control of individual sounds, keys to trigger individual drum sounds, and storage locations for a number of different rhythms. Most drum machines can also be controlled via MIDI.

### Digital sampler
A sampler is an electronic musical instrument that can record and store audio signal samples, generally recordings of existing sounds, and play them back at a range of pitches. However, "sampler" is sometimes used to describe instruments that store and play back samples but lack the capability to record them.

An early form of sampler was an instrument called the Mellotron (later Novatron), which used individual pre-recorded tape loops, one under each key on the keyboard. Mellotrons required a lot of maintenance, but had a characteristic sound that was used on many 1970s records by groups such as Yes.

The emergence of the digital sampler made sampling far more practical, and as samplers added progressively more digital processing to their recorded sounds, they began to merge into the mainstream of modern digital synthesizers. The first digital sampling synthesizer was the Australian-produced Fairlight CMI, first available in 1979.

Modern digital samplers use mostly digital technology to process the samples into interesting sounds. Akai pioneered many processing techniques, such as crossfade looping to eliminate glitches, and time stretch to shorten or lengthen samples without affecting pitch, and vice versa.

During the early 1990s, hybrid synthesizers began to emerge that used very short samples of natural sounds and instruments (usually the attack phase of the instrument) along with digital synthesis to create more realistic instrument sounds. Examples are Korg's M,01W and the later Triton and Trinity series, Yamaha's SY series, and the Kawaii K series of instruments.

The modern-day music workstation usually features an element of sampling, from simple playback to complex editing that matches all but the most advanced dedicated samplers.

### Sampling
Sampling refers to the act of taking a portion of one sound recording and reusing it as an instrument in a new recording. This is done with a sampler, which can either be a piece of hardware or a computer program on a digital computer. Similar to sampling is the technique of creating loops of magnetic tape with a reel-to-reel tape machine.

### Sound module
A sound module is an electronic musical instrument without a human-playable interface such as a keyboard, for example. Sound modules have to be "played" using an externally connected device.

**Software studios** *are the latest hot item. Rather than designing complex hookups of plugins, sequencers, and other music software, simply fire up one program that does it all: sampling, effects sequencing, and instruments. It may not be as powerful as the traditional sequencer/plug-in combo, but for many musicians it's more than enough to get the job done. Now available: Orion Pro, Storm, FruityLoops, and (free) Buzz (www. buzzmachines.com). The most famous of all is Propellerhead's Reason, with all the tools you need to make high-quality music plus a superb interface for under $600.*

The external device may be a controller, which provides the human-playable interface and may or may not produce sounds of its own, or a sequencer, which is computer hardware or software designed to play electronic musical instruments. Connections between sound modules, controllers, and sequencers are generally made with MIDI, which is a standardized protocol designed for this purpose.

### Synthesizer

A synthesizer is an electronic musical instrument designed to produce artificially generated sound, using techniques such as additive, subtractive, FM, and physical modeling synthesis to create sounds. Synthesizers create sounds through direct manipulation of electrical currents (as in analog synthesizers), mathematical manipulation of discrete values using computers (as in software synthesizers), or by a combination of both methods. In the final stage of the synthesizer, electrical currents are used to cause vibrations in the diaphragms of loudspeakers, headphones, etc. This synthesized sound is contrasted with recording of natural sound, where the mechanical energy of a sound wave is transformed into a signal which will then be converted back to mechanical energy on playback (though sampling significantly blurs this distinction).

### Recordable blank media

Recordable blank media comes in different formats, which can be purchased for duplicating or creating a tangible copy of an album. Formats include CDR/RW (Recordable CD), DVD, Diskettes, MINI-Disc, and audiotape. The cost of recordable blank media has drastically decreased over time, allowing consumers to make their own digital copies on CD and causing album sales to decrease. It has also provided a way for illegal street vendors to make high quality CD bootlegs that have been vigorously opposed by the recording industry. By daisy chaining or patching together recordable CD burners, bootleggers can produce thousands of CDs at a time.

*The average price of recordable CDs is now under 50¢ each.*

### Copy protection

Starting in early 2002, attempts were made by record
companies to market so-called *copy-protected* CDs.
These CDs rely on deliberate errors being introduced
into the data recorded on the disc. The intent is that
the error-correction in a music player will enable
music to be played as normal, while causing computer
CD-ROM drives to fail. However, not all current drives
fail, and copying software is being adapted to cope
with these damaged data tracks.

### Recordability

Compact discs cannot be easily recorded, as they
are manufactured by etching a glass plate and using
that plate to press metal. However, there are also CD-
recordable discs, which can be recorded by a laser
beam using a CD-R writer (most often on a computer,
though standalone units are also available), and can
be played on most CD players. CD-R recordings are
permanent and cannot be recorded more than once,
so the process is also called **burning** a CD. CD-RW is a
medium that allows multiple recordings on the same
disc over and over again. Many CD audio players
cannot read CD-RW discs, but more standalone DVD
players can read CD-RW than only CD-R discs. For
drives installed in computers, all current CD-ROM and
DVD-ROM drives can read and write CD-R and CD-RW
discs.

### CD-R

A CD-R (Compact Disk - Recordable) is a thin disc
made of polycarbonate with a 120 mm diameter,
which is mainly used to store music or data. However,
unlike conventional CD media, a CD-R has a core of
dye instead of metal. The first CD-Rs were produced
in 1997 by the companies Memorex, Maxell, and TDK.

A specially designed type of CD-ROM drive, called a
CD-R drive, CD burner, or CD writer can be used to
write CD-Rs. A laser is used to etch ("burn") small pits
into the dye so that the disc can later be read by the
laser in a CD-ROM drive or CD player. Once a section

***Many CD Burners***
*now cost less than
$100. You can search
for the low prices on
www.froogle.com.*

of a CD-R is written, it cannot be erased or rewritten, unlike a CD-RW. A CD-R can be recorded in multiple sessions.

### CD Burner

There was some incompatibility with CD-Rs and older CD-ROM drives. This was primarily due to the lower reflectivity of the CD-R disc. In general, CD drives marked as 8x or greater will read CD-R discs. Some DVD players will not read CD-Rs because of this change in reflectivity as well. A CD burner is an external writable CD-drive that can be attached to a computer. It lets you write and read files from a computer onto compact disk media, and is standard equipment in most new computers. The burner describes the process of the laser burning the organic dye substrate in the disk, creating a nonreflective pit signifying a bit state.

Burners can write CDs at multiple speeds. At 1x speed, for example, the CD spins at the same rate as the player reading it, taking you sixty minutes to record sixty minutes of data. At 2x it will take you half an hour, and so on.

***MIDI***, *developed in
the early 1980s—
allows musicians to
program a variety of
electronic musical
instruments to play
back a piece of music
all at once in real
time, rather than
recording each
instrument
separately and
mixing together later.*

### MIDI (Musical Instrument Digital Interface)

MIDI is a system designed to transmit information between electronic musical instruments. MIDI allows computers, synthesizers, sound cards, and drum machines to control one another, and to exchange system information. Though modern computer sound cards are MIDI-compatible and capable of creating realistic instrument sounds, the fact that sound cards' MIDI synthesizers have historically produced sounds of dubious quality has tarnished the image of a general purpose computer as a MIDI instrument. MIDI is almost directly responsible for bringing an end to the "wall of synthesizers" phenomenon in 1970s– 80s rock music concerts. Following the advent of MIDI, many synthesizers were released in rack-mount versions, enabling performers to control multiple instruments from a single keyboard. Another important effect of MIDI has been the development of hardware and computer-based sequencers, which can be used to record, edit, and play back performances.

### Sequencing

Music sequencing software runs entirely on personal computers. Sequencers come in two varieties: pure MIDI sequencers and MIDI/audio sequencers. Pure MIDI sequences only allow the recording, playing back, and editing of MIDI data. MIDI/audio sequencers can also sequence MIDI data alongside audio data.

### Sequencer

In the field of electronic music, a sequencer is a device that records and plays back control information for an electronic musical instrument such as a synthesizer. Earlier analog music sequencers used the control voltage/trigger interface, but have been replaced by digital sequencers for all practical purposes. A MIDI sequencer plays back MIDI events and MIDI control information at a specified number of beats per minute.

### Plug-ins

A plug-in is a computer program that can or must interact with another program to provide a certain, usually very specific, function. Real Time AudioSuite plug-ins are the proprietary software signal processors included with Pro Tools. They render effects in real time and are not a file-based process. The plug-ins utilize the host computer to render the effects as the session plays.

*In the computer world, a **plug-in** isn't something you stick into an electric socket, but it works something like that. It's more like a special addition to a computer program that adds some new capability—perhaps a special sound effect—into a program you already have.*

### Music workstation

A music workstation is a combination of two pieces of electronic music equipment:
1. sound generator, normally with a music keyboard
2. sequencer

The workstation is intended to provide a single piece of equipment that can be used to create music.

The sound generator is usually a synthesizer, which produces sounds by processing audio signals in electronic circuits (analog or digital), or a sampler, which produces sounds by replaying a stored recording of the sound (analog or digital).

The sounds produced by the sound generator will normally include drums and instrument sounds. The sequencer stores events like notes and controllers (pitch bend), and replays them into the sound generator, which then makes the music.

### Technics SL-1200

The Technics SL-1200 is a series of turntables manufactured by Matsushita under the brand name of Technics. As of 2004, the Technics SL-1200 MK2 was the industry standard turntable for DJ'ing and scratching, and is an improvement of the Technics SL-1200 first made in October 1972. The MK2, released in 1978, had several

improvements including the motor and casing. Since 1972, more than 3 million units have been sold.

### Scratching

Scratching is performed by moving a vinyl record back and forth with your hand while it is playing on a turntable, creating a distinctive sound that has come to be an almost universally recognized aspect of Hip-hop music.

# Recording & Manufacturing Processes

### Tracking (multitrack recording)

Tracking is the process of recording individual sounds or vocals on specific, individual tracks to be mixed together later. They may be recorded on digital or analog equipment, at the same time or different times, but they are kept separate until the mixing phase, when each track can be adjusted for volume and other sound parameters.

### Mixing

Through the process of mixing, each track's final and permanent volume level is determined and all of the digital effects (echoes, delays, reverbs) are added. The treble and bass are equalized. Some tracks are routed to the "left" side and some to the "right" to create stereo sound—an example of the **sweetening** process. What you hear after the mixing session is the final record.

### Mastering

Mastering is the last step before manufacturing. It is a process that sets the final loudness levels of the song's final mix. That's why you can usually play an album all the way through without having to adjust the loudness of individual songs. Many albums combine songs produced by various producers at different studios with different engineers.

Mastering gives a cohesive sound to the different tracks for listening pleasure and convenience. The final adjustments are  recorded onto a 2-track stereo CD or a 1630 (digital beta or dat, etc.). This final medium is sent to the manufacturing plants and is molded into metal and plastic parts.

### Master recordings (Masters)

The master recording is physically provided to and owned by the owner of the recording, regardless of its format (2" tape, digital format, Pro-Tools format on a removable drive, etc.). The owner has the right to market, manufacture, distribute, re-license, assign it, etc., as outlined in the recording contract.

## How to listen to your master/ reference CD

*When you get your music back from the mastering lab, don't just rush back to the studio where you mixed it for your first listen. As any record company executive knows, it's much less important what the record sounds like on the most expensive sound system than how it sounds on the least expensive sound system. Check it out on home systems, boom boxes, the car, clubs, etc. You're accustomed to hearing it in the studio, and it's going to sound different. But real-world sound is what's important. Take notes about what you hear. The mastering engineer can easily reproduce what was done before and make any changes you'd like.*

### Pressing

The master recording is transformed into physical "parts" which are used to duplicate the music— i.e., embed it into plastic or tape. The plant then prints it, inserts it into packaging, shrinkwraps it, and voila! The finished product ready to ship to distributors. Pressing may be a service provided by distributors, or a pressing plant can be hired.

### Soundtrack

A soundtrack is a musical compilation of songs inspired by a film or from a musical. Soundtracks typically include contributions by a single artist or by different artists. Over the years, soundtracks have made best seller status (i.e., *The Bodyguard* and *Saturday Night Fever*).

### Cover tune

A cover tune is a rearrangement or a remake of a previously recorded song. The basic structure is still the same but usually there is a new arrangement.

### Album snippets

Snippets are portions of songs that help give the consumer a preview of an artist's album. They are effective in creating awareness of a new and upcoming artist.

### Logo

Logos are registered or trademarked symbols used to identify the record label or the production company. Graphic artists are hired to create a logo that helps to *brand* the company.

# 5 Quick Tips for Improving Your Mixdown Masters

**1. *If you must compress the stereo output, make an alternate version with less or no compression.*** *Too much compression can restrict what's possible in mastering. It's good to make a version with peak limiting to see how your mix holds up when it's time to make the level hotter. Send both a limited and non-limited version to be mastered.*

**2. *Listen to your favorite commercial CDs in the control room to compare with your sound.*** *Use an "A–B" comparison of different sources and instantly level-match them so the comparison isn't just a volume contest.*

**3. *Be aware of the level of the lead vocals*** *from song-to-song. Listen again to your previous mixes.*

**4. *Allow for extra time to mix.*** *At this crucial stage, nothing is worse than running out of money and getting stuck with less than the best. Mixing is a crucial point in your project.*

**5. *Take breaks, have fun, enjoy the process.*** *Treat your mixing engineer to lunch or dinner. It will go a long way toward a fresh and pleasing experience.*

# *Timeline of Current*

**VINYL -** This analog technology is relatively obscure nowadays, except for club singles and record pool servicing. Most labels still manufacture vinyl 12-inch singles because many club DJs prefer them for their ability blend, scratch, and mix. Vinyl has proven to be the most reliable medium to store music—vinyl pressings 50 years old suffer very little loss of sound quality. CDs, which have been manufactured only for the past 20 years, seem to be storing music well, although we don't know for sure how they'll hold up over the long run.

*1948 to present*

**CASSETTE -** Another form of analog technology, audio cassettes came on the scene in the early 1960s. By 1982, cassettes outsold vinyl. Even today, cassettes are still used—Gospel and street artist music sell more cassettes than CDs. But as more and more automobiles are sold with CDs and MP3 players, and as CD burners and recordable CDs have become plentiful and cheap, cassettes are quickly becoming obsolete. Cassettes are a poor medium for storing music; tape edges fray after only a few years.

*1964 to present*

**COMPACT DISC-** CDs were one of the fastest-adopted technologies in history. Introduced in the early 80s, this digital format became the preferred music medium within a decade. By the '90s, many music fans were replacing entire collections of LPs with CDs. So far, factory-created CDs (made in multi-million-dollar "clean rooms") have proven to be a very reliable storage medium. However, CDs made with consumer equipment (i.e., $150 CD burner) have proven less reliable: readability may decline over just a few years.

*1983 to present*

# *Media Technologies*

***DAT*** (Digital Audio Tape) - First available for consumer usage in 1986 (long before anyone was burning CDs except billion-dollar factories), DAT was popular with recording artists because it made their digital music portable. For the same reason, DAT posed a big piracy risk to the recording industry, which fought to prevent its development. Today DAT is very popular, but for an entirely different usage: to back up computer systems and store digital data.

*1986 to present*

***MINIDISC***- Introduced in Japan in 1992, the MiniDisc became wildly popular there, but far less popular in America. The MiniDisc has near-CD sound, is virtually indestructible, and you can record on the same MiniDisc thousands of times. Electronics companies and record labels hoped consumers would again replace their music collections by switching to this compact format.

*1992 to present*

***AUDIO DVD*** - The audio DVD technology developed in the late '90s is different than video DVDs, and requires different (and costly) playback equipment. The development of DVD audio provides home theater sound as well as regular stereo sound, but until we can play audio DVDs on our regular DVD or CD players, are we really interested?

*1990s to ?*

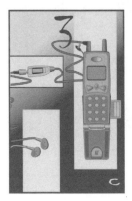

## Music as Digital Code
*(Music you can't hold in your hand)*

**WAVE, AIFF FILES** Uncompressed digital audio files about eight times larger than MP3s—too large to download, but just right to edit high quality music in many programs on your PC.

**MP3 AND MP4** The MP3 format has become the standard for transmitting music over the Internet, thanks to its tiny file size. At only 12 percent of the size of standard audio files (WAVE, AIFF, etc), MP3 files still retain about 90 percent of the sound quality. They are examples of a new form of digital compression that makes music files smaller than ever without sacrificing much sound quality. No doubt music files will become even smaller and pack in even higher quality as new **codecs** are discovered ("codec" stands for "compression-decompression"). The MP4 format was developed by Apple as a secure, higher-quality format to sell digital music through its iTunes stores. MP3s and MP4s can be played and stored on computer hard drives, removable drives, and MP3 players, including the Rio and Apple iPod.

1101010010100101
1010100111011010
0101010100010111
0100010001101010
101001010101010
1110110101010101
1000101111010001
0011010100101001
1010101001110110
010101010100010
1110100010001101
100101001010101
1001110110101010
010100010111010
0100011010100101
0101010101001110
1010101010101000
0111101000100011
101001010010101
101001110110110
010101000101110
0001000110101001
1001010101010011
0110101010101010
0101111010001000
101001010100010
010100111010101
101010100001111
1000100011010100
010010101010100
1101101010101010
000101110100010
0110101001010010

## JUKEBOXES

*...Then*

*...and Now*

**The concept**

**Approved by A&R**

**Budget allocated**

**How Music Goes from Concept to Recorded Product**

**Product recorded**

**Product mixed**

**Product mastered**

**Product duplicated**

**Product delivered to distributor**

# 3.

................

# Contracts: For
# Better or for Worse

Recording contracts in the record business are considered a "necessary evil." Although you might think you can maintain a good working relationship based on your word or a handshake, you may be risking hundreds of thousands or millions of dollars if the other party doesn't remember that word or handshake the way you do. While verbal agreements are enforceable, they are much more difficult to enforce than agreements in writing. But why is a lawyer needed?

As we all know, handshake agreements work fine—until some real money and fame come into play, in other words, until you encounter something you weren't expecting. Suddenly, relationships begins to change. Why is one person making more money than the others? People begin to forget their promises and obligations, or say they didn't know that such and such would happen, or they would have acted differently. Or that one party has lied about an important fact, or one party has taken advantage of the other. But lawyers know all the bad stuff that can happen, and they can prevent it from happening to you.

The record business is *seductive*— it lures people from all walks of life, including those who are successful in all kinds of businesses and professions. People who

## What is a contract?

*A contract is an **agreement** between two or more persons (**parties**) that creates an obligation to do or not to do a particular thing by a specific date. The contract may be expressed (either written or oral) or implied from circumstances. Typically, the remedy for breach of contract is an award of money (**damages**) to restore the injured party to the economic position the party expected from performance of the contract. Technically, a valid contract requires an offer and an acceptance of that offer, and a form of consideration (money or something of value). Both sides should benefit from a contract.*

## Recording Contract Basics

**1. Length**: How long will the label own the rights to your master recording? Usually the company wants rights to several future albums in case your first album is successful.

**2. Creative Control**: Most artists want rights to choose the material and style.

**3. Cash Advance**: It may be a long time before you see your first royalty check, so you will need an **advance** — a portion of the recording budget— to live on until the album is finished and you can start touring or earning money other ways.

**4. Recoupment**: How will the label deduct from your royalties to cover costs of airplay, promotion, artist development, and your video? For some artists, the label may take the whole cost of the video from the artist's royalties; another artist may pay for only half the video.

**5. Royalty Rate**: How much will you earn from every record sold?

join forces to chase stardom and fame find that getting a little taste of it can do a lot of damage to the "team" relationships. Those who give up future choices in order to get an exclusive contract with a specific person or company may later regret their choices. As you learn more about the business, you too will wish you had made different choices, signed different contracts, and picked better advisors. We have seen this happen many, many times in the record business with all types of recording artists.

We're seeing more and more major artists rebelling against major labels. Artists such as Courtney Love and George Michael have tried to get out of their contracts because they did not feel they were treated fairly by record labels. New strategies developed by major artists and their high-paid entertainment attorneys have allowed artists to renegotiate their contracts, or be released

from them in order to obtain more favorable agreements from their labels or find deals with other labels.

## Basic Disagreements That Lead to Agreements

How is it that an artist or group that barely makes enough to survive can keep the faith in their future— but when some money finally starts to kick in, the group breaks up? Simple: because someone feels cheated. Because the guy who does all the grunt work regrets that he agreed to the same share of royalties as the other members. Because one group member makes twice as much as the others since he writes most of the songs. Because the producer gets more royalties than any of the group members—who talked them into that? And, down the road, a hit artist with an enormous fan base realizes he no longer needs the record label that continues to take take the lion's share of his record's profits.

Artists rarely consider the millions of dollars spent by the record label to market and promote their recordings. The artist realizes he has the ability to sell millions of records to millions of fans, although he forgets that those fans didn't exist until the record company spent millions of dollars to expose the artist's music and image to millions of people.

Let's face the facts: we cannot sell records to the consumer unless the consumer has heard them or knows about the artist. This is why the recording contract is necessary to protect the investment of both parties: recording artist and record label.

Several kinds of contracts are needed to define all the principal roles in a music project. If you're the record company, you want a contract that binds the artist to your label exclusively—in other words, the artist cannot record for another label during the term of the contract. Since you put up all the money to record the music and promote the product, you need a guarantee that you will receive the profits from the product you financed.

If you are a producer, you will need an agreement between you and the record company that will define your obligations and share of the profits and those of the label. If you are a songwriter writing with a partner, you will need a co-publishing contract that spells out what percentages of profits you and your partner will receive.

Many parts of a contract can be customized to fit your situation, generally based on how many records the label thinks you can sell. An artist that is expected to sell big, based on their sales history, gets privileges and royalty rates higher than a brand new artist. But what it boils down to is the terms and conditions that are *agreed to by both parties.* You'd be surprised at the

*Everyone says I should read the contract before I sign it. But if I can't understand it, why bother?*

**DO THIS:**
*Don't be afraid to ask your attorney to explain the parts you don't understand. After all, he works for you, not vice versa. Ask your lawyer to break down the contract into short bullet points in a 1- or 2-page summary.*

**BUT NOT THIS:**
*Don't let the label see your paranoia about not getting everything you can possibly get. There's a fine line between being cautious and killing the record deal because the label realizes you're incompetent and hard to deal with. Let your attorney deal with the label—that's what you pay him for.*

# What Is the "Seven-Year Rule"?

California's Labor Code Section 2855 (the "Seven Year Statute") limits the time a person can be held to a personal services contract to seven years. **Subsection B**— added In 1987—provided a limited exception for recording contracts. Recording artists are now the only personal service workers in California who cannot take advantage of Labor Code 2855 and freely negotiate for better terms or seek new agreements after seven years.

The problem is that an average recording contract requires seven albums released approximately 18 to 24 months apart. During that time, the artist and label must write, produce, tour, promote, and market the album. If the album is successful, the next album may be delayed. This makes it virtually impossible for artists to fulfill their contracts within seven years.

The California Senate has held three hearings on recording industry practices. The first was on California's Seven-Year Rule and the exception of recording contracts. As a result, legislation was introduced to repeal Subsection B. RAC (Recording Artists Coalition) and the RIAA negotiated but failed to produce an agreement. The bill was put on hold for upcoming legislative sessions.

Following California's lead, other states are considering limiting the length of personal service contracts. The Speaker of the New York Assembly introduced legislation, and other proposals are under discussion in Georgia, Texas, Florida, and Tennessee.

## Senate Bill 1246

RAC, AFTRA, and the AFM strongly support California Senate Bill 1246 to repeal subsection (B).

RAC maintains that the discriminatory practice of singling out recording artists is inherently unfair.

Recording artists are generally unsure how the seven-year rule affects them. Record companies know that it is highly unlikely artists will be able to deliver seven or eight albums in seven years. The demands they place on their artists, including touring to promote albums, video shoots, and other marketing chores, is overwhelming and time-consuming. Many artists with successful records are forced to tour to support their albums. The record companies won't allow the release of another album because they don't want it to compete with the already successful album. In some cases it can be years before recording artists have the opportunity to write, record, and release another record. The resulting "catch 22" makes it impossible for recording artists to fulfill their delivery obligation within seven years.

differences between recording contracts. Remember: if you don't ask, you won't receive.

## Is your attorney worth $300 an hour?

To get the best possible deal you need an experienced entertainment attorney who specializes in the record business. Entertainment attorneys may

be more expensive than other kinds of attorneys, but they can be worth their weight in gold. Investing in an experienced music attorney is your best insurance against being deprived of money you earn. Nine times out of ten, an entertainment attorney will find ways to add extras to the contract that the record company will approve. But you must choose an attorney who specializes in music. It won't help to hire your family attorney or a criminal attorney to review a recording contract. They're not always up on the newest ways to extract the most money from record companies or how the changing laws of your state affect you. Think about it: would you hire an entertainment attorney to fight a criminal case?

Experienced attorneys know how much a label can afford to pay you. The rules change very quickly and attorneys have to stay plugged into the information pipelines to know which major labels are willing to give a million-dollar deal to another new act. Although labels try to keep that information confidential, music attorneys make it their business to know such "secrets," and use them as leverage to ask for more money and other perks.

### Don't Think "Demo"

*The record industry is mostly owned by large conglomerates, whose music departments tend to be the smallest divisions. They're headed by accountants and lawyers, who are skilled in ensuring bottom-line profits, but not in identifying hit sounds. They didn't get into the record business because they loved music, but because they were made responsible for the music division in a corporate restructure. So they may not have the musical sensitivity to hear a demo, know how to fix it, or whether a live horn session will add pizzazz. Instead of looking for innovative, new sounds, they go for cookie cutter formulas.*

***Your music must sound like a hit for them to "get it." So treat your demo as the real thing at all times. Finished product is what big labels want.***

## Can't I just get a copy of the form and fill it in?

*As one big-time L.A. record business lawyer said, "The form is free, but filling in the blanks is very expensive." But for those who want to give it a try, consider 101 Music Business Contracts. I do not recommend this company over others, but you get all 101 contracts for around $100—or less, if you want to download them all. The contracts come in a word editing program so you can change a few words or every word. And they will at least look neat and professional.*

**www.order-yours-now.com/**

**www.musiccontracts.com/**

# The Nuts and Bolts of a Recording Contract Negotiation

**Contract** is any promise or set of promises made by one party to another for the breach of which the law provides a remedy. The promise or promises may be expressed (either written or oral) or may be implied from circumstances. Typically, the remedy for breach of contract is an award of money damages intended to restore the injured party to the economic position that he or she expected from performance of the promise or promises.

**License** is an agreement giving someone permission to do or use something. The owner of a song, for example, may require that a license be accepted as a condition for being allowed to reproduce the copyrighted work.

**Negotiation** is the process between persons or parties to resolve disputes, agree upon courses of action, bargain for individual or collective advantage, and attempt to craft outcomes which serve their mutual interests.

A typical record label is in the business of acquiring rights to a master recording forever or for a very long time. The artist, on the other hand, wants to own his masters someday. The label will want rights to several albums and options to extend the contract period in order to take advantage of an artist who becomes a star. The artist will want the most flexible contract so he's not tied to the same deal forever.

The label wants enough control over the music to ensure that it has a "hit" sound. But the artist thinks she should have creative control—she's the creative talent, not the label executive.

The artist will need money to live on while she creates her album, in the form of a (big as possible) cash advance deducted from the recording budget.

The record company wants to risk as little money as possible until they know whether they have a hit record or not.

The label will want the right to recoup their cash outlay (i.e., get the money back that they paid to finance the recording and marketing) from the artist's royalties. Nowadays, record labels are also recouping the costs of videos (all or part), radio airplay promotion, and marketing. All these key points are subject to negotiation. The artist wants to keep as much of their royalties as possible.

All these points are subject to negotiation. Nothing is written in stone.

## What Other Kinds of Contracts Might Be Needed?

**Producer's contract:** A producer's contract defines his or her percentage share (points) and the break-even point (how many records must be sold to pay back the recording budget to the record company before the producer earns royalties). Depending on what the producer and label agree to, a producer may get paid from the very first record sold. The producer's contract also defines who pays the producer. In some recording contracts, the artist is responsible for paying the producer. In these cases, the producer may request a "direct to pay" agreement, which makes the record company— not the artist—responsible to pay him.

**Production deal agreement** A producer/production company is in the business of developing, recording, and producing recordings that will be manufactured and "worked" by large record labels. The difference between a record label and a production company is that the record label manufactures, promotes, markets, and distributes product. In a production deal, the record company agrees to purchase a specific

### What is a "Key Man clause"?

*In a contract, a "Key Man Clause" insures that a specific person or persons will remain in place in the organization (label, management firm, talent agency, etc.) or the recording artist will be freed from the contract.*

*The clause is used primarily when a specific executive is instrumental to the artist's career, or the artist does not feel comfortable without his or her guidance. An example is Arista recording artist Alicia Keys, who named Clive Davis as her Key Man. When Davis left Arista, Keys—still an unknown act—exercised the clause, ended her contract with Arista, and moved to Davis's new label, J Records. She eventually recorded a multi-Grammy-winning, multi-platinum debut album, which became one of the biggest sellers of all time.*

**Can an "artist showcase" help get a recording deal?**

*An effective method for drumming up interest in a new project is the new artist showcase, which is particularly effective for artists that are visually exciting. Many record labels, performance rights organizations (BMI, ASCAP, SERAC), and music conferences (Impact, NARM, BRE) have new artist showcases. For a small registration fee, new acts are given the opportunity to perform before music executives.*

number of master recordings from the production company. Production companies are responsible for managing budgets and delivering product on time. Usually each project is entirely funded by the record label and the artist is under contract to the record company through the production company. The production company receives a royalty directly from the record company. In some cases the production company is responsible for finding artists for the record label.

**Imprint deal** is basically the same as a production deal, but the record label agrees to display the production company logo alongside the label logo on all product sold or advertised.

**Joint venture** is similar to a production deal, except that the label (which finances the project) and the producer/production company split the profits after deducting expenses. Royalties are paid as usual.

## Please Listen to My Demo ...
### (or How to Shop a Record Production or Publishing Deal)

In the past, it was common for anyone seeking a recording contract, publishing or production deal to have a demo (demonstration tape): a barebones recording usually made on a low budget, with low-grade, incomplete versions of the proposed project or songs. Because of the high expense of recording and hiring musicians, studio, engineer, etc., it was prohibitively expensive to present a finished product that fairly represented the artist, producer, or song-writer. So when a songwriter would "demo" a song to a company, it was common for the demo to consist of just piano and vocals. Many record deals were signed as the result of a skinny 4-track demo tape that showed the potential of a writer, producer, or artist.

However, with the rapid advancement of music technology, the demo tape has become obsolete. With the use of digital sequencers, digital recording and computers, drum machines, and other electronic gadgets, the artist,producer, or songwriter has the ability to complete a master recording in the comfort of his home. As a result, record labels, managers, and artists have grown accustomed to hearing a finished product, not a barebones demo. If you present a demo tape to a record label or artist or publisher, it will demonstrate that you are an amateur. The record company wants to hear what the finished product will sound like.

## What can a logo do for me?

*Your logo is a symbol that identifies your record label or production company. This is important in branding your company and your artist, and it becomes more valuable the more hits you have. A logo associated with a hit artist or sound can be applied to all kinds of manufactured goods—from t-shirts and belt buckles to entire clothing lines—that have instant recognition, credibility, and "hipness" to potential buyers. Make sure to hire a good graphic artist to create a logo that reflects your company. Eventually, have the logo trademarked or registered.*

When producing or arranging vocals, mix to the best of your abilities and use the best vocals you can manage. Treat every aspect like it's the finished thing, even if you intend to re-produce it at a later time, or replace digitized instruments with live musicians, or bring in higher-quality equipment, or mix on a pro console. The only enhancements that can be forgiven in the presentation of product are vocals and mixing on a pro mixer. If you are an artist seeking a recording deal, try to finish the whole project. This is attractive to record labels because it shows you are self-sufficient, competent, determined, self-contained, and can manage a budget. Such factors increase your chances of getting a better deal by giving them a better idea of how much more you may be capable of accomplishing.

**Master purchase deal** A masterful music presentation that shows off a complete album can turn into a goldmine—a master purchase deal instead of a recording deal. In a master purchase, the label buys the music master as basically complete. It doesn't have to fund a long, uncertain recording process, or pay large advances and producers' and artists' royalties. The ownership is transferred to the buyer, although royalties will be paid to the artist, songwriters, etc., on each record sold. After all, you haven't risked their money for your project, and you are rewarded for that.

If you have your eyes on a master purchase deal, the best

**How are recording contracts negotiated?**

Record company's legal department prepares first draft and sends it to the artist's attorney for renegotiation, comments, and changes.

Attorney sends contract back to label with comments.

Label makes agreed changes; artist and label sign final contract.

thing to do is try to get local support for your record—such as local radio stations and record stores—after you finish the project. Most radio stations have an open call day when anyone can meet with the music or program director and present product and solicit them for support or airplay. Most local radio stations want to support local artists. Because of the success of recent home-made hits, radio people understand that desktop technology makes music good enough to put on the air, which makes radio folk feel like they're supporting their own.

If local radio stations won't add your record to their playlist, see if they'll put it in a "pump it or dump it" event—a battle of the bands decided by listeners calling in and voting on which records the station should add to its playlist. This can prove very effective. Most labels have regional reps in major cities and surrounding areas that closely watch for regional records that get airplay without a record deal. In other words, if your record is hot, the label will find you. Believe me—this works. Nellie was a regional act out of St. Louis and has now sold 16 million records worldwide.

For writers seeking publishing deals, try submitting your work to various publishers. Publishers are more in the business of finding you, but unfortunately for new writers, publishers are more likely to sign writers who already have record deals or producers who have production deals. Like the record business, the music publishing business has also become highly profit-driven and far less creative-driven. They'd much rather sign an artist with other deals in place because they're more likely to get a return on their investment. In past years, publishers signed unknown writers they believed had potential, and helped the writers develop and find songs. Today, this rarely happens. Now music publishers wait for record and production deals to be in place because it ensures that they can get money for publishing rights. Music publishers are becoming loan companies that advance you money from your future royalties, but charge you 30 percent for administering your songs. Really they're just loaning you your own money. The only good reason to do a publishing deal is to get an advance or song-plugging for your catalog of songs. So, if you can, it's better to retain your publishing rights.

Publishers also exploit the songs as much as possible —that is, find others to record your songs—and some are very talented and have wide contacts in that area.

**Work for hire** is a term that means the author no longer owns the work, but transfers rights to it for a fee. The author is then no longer eligible for further royalties or ownership participation. This must be agreed to in advance and noted on the copyright forms. It is best to have a written agreement because we all know that when records become hits, people seem to forget previous arrangements.

**Re-recording restriction** is a clause in a recording agreement that prevents an artist from re-recording the material he records for his current label for another label, usually for a period of 5-10 years. It is designed to protect the label's investment in marketing and promotion. It prevents an artist who leaves a label—perhaps under unhappy circumstances—from going to another label and re-recording all his hits for the second label to sell.

**Exclusive** describes an artist who is under a recording agreement and not allowed (without the permission of the label) to record, or use their likeness or image for any outside purpose while under the recording agreement.

**Recoupment** is the repayment out of royalties of any monies advanced to the artist, producer, or songwriter.

### Points
Jargon for percentage used, referring to royalties. Usually one point is one percent.

### Sides
This is industry jargon referring to a single song; they are sometimes called *tracks*.

### A-side protection
When the producer is guaranteed that one of his productions will be on the *A* side of the first single as opposed to side *B*.

### Entertainment law
A general term for a mix of more traditional categories of law with a focus on providing legal services to the entertainment industry. Entertainment law often involves questions of employment law (employment contracts for talent and production personnel), labor law (negotiating and arbitrating with trade unions), immigration issues regarding foreign talent, securities law regarding promoting properties, security interests, payment and collection of royalties, agency, intellectual property, and insurance law. Much of the work of an entertainment law practice is transaction based: drafting contracts, negotiation, and mediation. Some situations may lead to litigation or arbitration.

### Music contract software and Websites
There are software programs that have ready-made contracts. They come in several versions of computer word processing programs, which allow the opportunity to make changes to a legal document to fit your specific needs. Using one of these programs will give you a clean, neat professional looking document that will look as if it came straight from a top entertainment lawyer's office.

Take a look at **www.order-yours-now.com** and **www.musiccontracts.com** for ordering music contract software.

# BOOKING AGREEMENT (Example)

THIS CONTRACT, entered into on this __th day of _____, 200_, is for the personal services of the Musician(s) for the performance described below. The undersigned Employer and the undersigned Musician(s) agree and contract as follows:

1. NAME OF MUSICIAN(S):

2. NUMBER OF MUSICIAN(S):

3. NAME AND ADDRESS OF PLACE OF PERFORMANCE:

4. DATE(S) OF PERFORMANCE:

5. TIME(S) OF PERFORMANCE:

6. WAGE AGREED UPON:

7. DEPOSIT:

8. PAYMENT OF BALANCE TO _____ MADE IN U.S. CURRENCY OR CERTIFIED CHECK AT THE END OF PERFORMANCE.

9. ADDITIONAL TERMS:

10. This contract constitutes a complete and binding agreement between the Employer and the Musician(s). AGENT acts only as agent and assumes no responsibility as between the Employer and the Musician(s).

11. In case of breach of this contract by Employer, the Employer agrees to pay the amount stated in Section 6 as mitigated damages, plus reasonable attorney's fees, court costs, and legal interest.

13. The Employer agrees to be responsible for harm, loss, or damage of any kind to Musician(s) person or property while located at the place of performance (Section 3 herein).

14. The persons signing for Employer and the Musician(s) agree to be personally, jointly and severally liable for the terms of this contract.

_____

for Musician(s)


_____

for Employer

# ASSIGNMENT OF COPYRIGHT (Example)

KNOW ALL MEN BY THESE PRESENTS, the undersigned assignor,

Name:
Address:
City:
State:
Zip:
Telephone:

for and in consideration of the sum of _____ ($____.00) and other valuable consideration, receipt of which is hereby acknowledged, does hereby assign, transfer and set over to the assignee,

Name:
Address:
City:
State:
Zip:
Telephone:

Its successors and assigns forever, all of its rights, title and interest in and to the musical composition now entitled:



written and composed by _____ together with any and all assignor's existing copyrights therein throughout the United States and the world, and any and all assignor's rights of every kind, nature or description attaching to or which may attach to said musical composition and/or embraces or included in the copyright thereof in the United States and entire world, which said composition the undersigned was originally assigned on _____, 200_, and was registered with the Copyright Office of the United States of America on _____, under Copyright Entry, Class E, Copyright Number _____. The form U registration is registered on _____ in Volume _____, page _____.

IN WITNESS WHEREOF, the undersigned has executed the foregoing instrument on this _____ day of _____ 200_.

ASSIGNEE: By: _____
Name:
Address:
City:
State:
Zip:

WITNESS: By: _____
Name:
Address:
City:
State:
Zip:

# ARTIST–MANAGER AGREEMENT (Example)

1. This is an agreement made this          day of                    200__,
between the undersigned MANAGER and the undersigned ARTIST.

2. The ARTIST has signed a recording contract with the following RECORD
COMPANY:
and the date of the contract was:                              , 200__.

3. In this agreement RECORD COMPANY promised to make royalty payments
to ARTIST.

4. ARTIST promises to pay to MANAGER the following percentage of the
amounts received by ARTIST from RECORD COMPANY:

5. ARTIST promises to make the payments to MANAGER as soon as the check
from the RECORD COMPANY is received by ARTIST.

6. ARTIST promises to send all royalty statements (or copies) and other communications (or copies) from RECORD COMPANY to MANAGER.

7. ARTIST hereby instructs his bookkeepers and accountants to make available for inspection and copying the RECORD COMPANY contract and all statements rendered by the RECORD COMPANY to the ARTIST.

8. This agreement does not cover and is not intended to cover any agreement
between the RECORD COMPANY and anyone else (including the ARTIST and
the MANAGER) concerning song publishing and mechanical licenses. In the
event either is entitled to share in songwriting and/or publishing rights
and/or royalties, a separate agreement will cover that aspect.

9. ARTIST hereby requests, instructs, authorizes and empowers RECORD COM-
PANY to pay said percentage directly to MANAGER.

10. The duration of this agreement commences as of the date of the contract
between ARTIST and RECORD COMPANY, and shall continue as long as ARTIST
is entitled to monies from RECORD COMPANY.

IN WITNESS WHEREOF we have entered into this written agreement as of the
date above written.

MANAGER:_____

WITNESS:_____


ARTIST:_____

DATE:_____


WITNESS:_____

DATE:_____

# CO-PUBLISHING AGREEMENT (Example)

CO-PUBLISHING AGREEMENT made this      day of                              200__,
in                                by the First Party:
                                  and the Second Party:


FIRST PARTY AND SECOND PARTY AGREE to co-publish together a musical
composition entitled:
                    , words and music written by:


1. First Party and Second Party agree to CO-PUBLISH the composition on a
fifty/fifty (50/50) basis: First Party to receive fifty (50%) percent, and Second
Party to receive fifty (50%) percent of any and all of the publishing receipts
of said composition, SUBSEQUENT TO PAYMENT of all writer royalties; costs
of COPYRIGHT and USAGE REGISTRATION; printing and any and all miscella-
neous, normal expenses incurred on behalf of said composition. Any extraor-
dinary expenses will not be incurred by either party without the written consent of the other; (i.e., advertising, publicity, promotional expenses).

2. Public Performance Rights in and to the composition will be assigned
to and licensed by (BROADCAST MUSIC, INC. BMI) is here authorized to pay
directly to each of the publishers the following: (a) First Party, 50%; (b) Second
Party, 50%.

3. The composition is to be copyrighted in the joint names of the parties
hereto, and the composition's joint ownership, under the terms of this
agreement, shall be for the life of the copyright and of any renewal of the
copyright and of any renewal terms anywhere in the world. Sheet music,
folios, record labels, orchestrations, and all other printed material concerning
the composition shall bear the names of both publishers.

4. Second Party agrees that First Party shall issue all licenses for the
mechanical reproduction, and synchronization uses of said composition
throughout the world, and for sub-publication rights to said composition
throughout the world on behalf of both parties.

5. It is further agreed that First Party shall be held accountable to Second
Party and the composer(s), and First Party agrees to make statements and
payments to Second Party and composer(s), within forty-five (45) days after

June 30th and December 31st of each calendar year.

FIRST
PARTY:_____

WITNESS:_____

SECOND
PARTY:_____

WITNESS:_____

# JOIN T  VENTURE  AGREEMENT  (Example)

_____

(Publisher)


_____

(Record Company)


_____

(Record Distributor)


The undersigned, desiring to enter into a joint venture, agree as follows:

I. The name of the joint venture shall
be:_____


2. The character of the business shall
be:_____


(a)  the publishing of music;
(b)  the production of phonograph record masters and phonograph records;
(c)  the promotion and distribution of phonograph records; and
(d)  all other business necessary and related thereto.

3. The location of the principal place of business shall be:


4. The name and place of residence of each of the undersigned is:


_____


_____


_____


_____

_____

_____

_____

5. Each of the undersigned shall contribute cash and property, and shall receive percentages of the net profit of the joint venture as follows:

| Name | % of Net Profit | Cash | Property |
| --- | --- | --- | --- |

Losses shall be shared in the same ratios as net profit.

6. Each of the undersigned may make additional contributions to, or withdrawals from, the capital of the joint venture, as may from time to time be agreed upon by all the partners.

7. The joint venture shall continue as long as the undersigned desire.

8. In the event of retirement, expulsion, bankruptcy, death or insanity of a member of the joint venture, the remaining members shall have the right to continue the business of the joint venture under the same name by themselves or in conjunction with any other person or persons whom they may select.

9. The members of the joint venture have the right to admit additional

members by unanimous decision only.

IN WITNESS WHEREOF, the undersigned members of the joint venture have hereunto set their hands this day:

_____.


_____(Publisher)

_____(Record Company)

_____(Record Distributor)

# 4.

· · · · · · · · · · · · · · · ·

# Ins and Outs of Music Publishing

Publishing is an example of a what can be called a "nickel-and-dime" business. But over the long run, this particular nickel-and-dime business is likely to earn you more revenue than record sales.

Publishing started out as the right to print and sell sheet music—even before there were records. Nowadays publishing refers more to the noncreative ownership of a composition. The writer of the song can either retain publishing rights or assign them to anyone he wishes—such as a music publisher. Typically, the publisher owns half the song and the writer owns half.

What does the music publisher do for its share? For one thing, the publisher may give you a cash advance against your song's future earnings. For example: a publisher is often willing to advance you up to 13.5 times a year's projected earnings. The publisher usually does all the paperwork in collecting publishing royalties and making sure they're correct. The publisher may also try to persuade other artists or producers to record your song ("plug" your song) or get your songs placed in movies.

### Licensing

By issuing someone a license, you are giving permission to use your song. Once the song has been recorded and publicly distributed, a different kind of licensing kicks in— compulsory licensing. Now, everyone who wants to record the song can do so without your permission. However, the user is required by law to pay you a statutory royalty rate, notify you that they're going to release it, and send

### How do songs earn royalties?

*Songs earn royalties when you give permission (in a process called **licensing**) to use your song, or when automatic permission is granted in return for payment. There are two kinds of song licensing:*

### Mechanical license

*is the licensing of copyrighted musical compositions for use on CDs, records, tapes, and certain digital configurations.*

### Statutory license

*allows a radio station to broadcast your song. A station pays an annual licensing fee that is split among all the songs it plays.*

you monthly royalty statements. They are not allowed to make any changes to the words or melody or change the "fundamental character of the song" without the copyright owner's approval. If the song is changed, it is considered a ***derivative work***. Record companies rarely use compulsory licensing because they don't want to have to provide monthly royalty statements. Instead, they go to the copyright owner and get a direct license so they can negotiate the terms more freely.

### What is a license?
*When you give permission for someone to use something that belongs to you, that permission is a form of a license. A license is usually a privilege that requires payment in return and lasts only a specific amount of time.*

Another type of licensing is for recorded performances. A performance (recording) owned by one party can be leased to another party for a period of time in exchange for a royalty or fee. Licensing is also how songs are used as samples and become part of compilations, movie soundtracks, ring tones, video games, and TV commercials (i.e., Bob Seger's "Like a Rock" commercials for Chevy trucks).

In recent years, licensing fees have generated millions of dollars worldwide. Now there's big licensing in electronic video games that include music. For instance, the game *NBA Live* earned an RIAA platinum award. One song used in a TV commercial can bring $45,000 to $700,000 in royalties to an artist and record company.

Video placements—songs on video games—can fetch from $2,000 to $25,000 for a new artist. TV and movie tie-ins still produce the lion's share of licensing. Last year $1.5 billion was earned this way.

### Co-publishing agreement
In a co-publishing agreement, two or more parties share rights to a song, either because they wrote the song together or because one assigned the rights of the song. This type of agreement specifies who owns what part of the song. It's not necessarily a creative agreement; you can give (or assign) your ownership to anybody you wish. And that party can collect royalties from the song for years to come.

# How a Song's Royalties Are Divided

**Songwriter's share: 50% of all income**

**Publisher's share: 50% of all income**

**So if total income is $1**

**Songwriter's share: 50 percent of $1 = 50¢**

**Publisher's share: 50 percent of $1 = 50¢**

### Shared copyright

If you write the lyrics to a song and your buddy writes the music, then you each own 50 percent of the song. You don't own all of the lyrics and your buddy doesn't own all of the music—you each own 50 percent of the total song, music, lyrics and all. This means you can't give someone exclusive rights to the song on your own if you have a fight with your buddy.  And, if you make any money on the song, half of that money must go to your partner.

Other forms of shared copyrights come into play when you or your publisher (typically you give control of the song's copyright to the publisher) sign over a portion of the copyright to another publisher for a sampled composition—a song that uses a portion of another song.

### Mechanical license

A mechanical license covers "hard" copies of the songs that are sold, such as CDs, cassettes, and albums. The federal government sets the payment rate annually for this portion of the copyright. The copyright owner (songwriter) grants the license to a manufacturer, who pays him on every copy sold. A songwriter can issue his own mechanical license to the label, or let someone else do it—such as the Harry Fox Agency, which handles about 90 percent of mechanical licenses. Fox will also send the royalties to the song owner and may conduct an audit to make sure the royalties are calculated correctly.

### Sampling made simple

Sampling refers to taking a portion of one sound recording and reusing it in a new recording. A sample is extracted with a digital sampler, which can be either hardware or a software program. Sampling requires a license from the song owner and, if the actual performance is used, from the owner of the master recording—usually the record company.

Sampling has become a very lucrative business for publishers—so big that publishers are now putting out sampling CDs that producers can sample from directly for potential licensing opportunities.

Most legal experts believe the issue of digital sampling was resolved in 1991, when a federal district court ruled that Biz Markie's use of a few notes from the chorus of Gilbert O'Sullivan's hit song "Alone Again, Naturally" amounted to copyright infringement. In addition to citing the Ten Commandments ("Thou shalt not steal"), the judge barred any further sale of Biz Markie's album and referred the matter to the U.S. Attorney's office for possible criminal prosecution. Another court later ruled that sampling phrases like "ooh," "move," and "free your body" may also be enough to find copyright infringement.

One of the most notable samples of all time is Puff Daddy's use of Sting's "Every Breath You Take" in "I'll Be Missing You." Sting received 100 percent of the royalties from that song. It is an example of when the portion of music sampled is so significant that it's considered to be a cover tune, the copyright owner retains 100 percent of the copyright and receives 100 percent of the mechanical license and airplay royalties.

Most publishing companies rely on clearance companies to clear the samples and make sure that all the legal bases are covered. Typically, the copyright owner and the sample user agree to split the royalty 50/50 when using a musical track that's lifted from the sample and the artist sings a new melody and lyrics over the sample. That's how the artist and copyright owner usually balance it. Most publishers won't take less than 20 percent ownership no matter how small the sample. Occasionally, if a sample is used only in an intro, they may go lower than the 20 percent.

### Obtaining a sampling clearance
To legally sample a song, you need to obtain

### Clearing Samples Yourself

*You may decide to obtain a sample license yourself. To clear samples, you write to the record company and to the publisher of the sampled song. ASCAP or BMI will likely have the publisher's current address.*

*In your letter, ask for a quote for a clearance fee, and identify the song you are sampling and how much is used. Don't forget to include a tape of the original song, as well as a copy of your unreleased song using the sample.*

permission from the copyright holder of the sound recording (usually the record company) and the copyright holder of the composition (usually the song's publisher). Permission from the owner should also be sought when sampling a television show or motion picture.

Artists should obtain permission from all copyright owners before any song containing a sample is distributed publicly. Waiting until after your record is distributed can result in lost income, expensive legal fees, and the removal of your record from the market. Releasing your record before obtaining clearances also reduces your bargaining power if you later attempt to negotiate a sample license.

### *How to clear a sample*

Music attorneys often clear samples, although they can be relatively expensive. Clearance agencies are usually cheaper, and many are familiar with licensing samples. Record companies can also clear samples for their artists, but the cost of negotiating and obtaining clearances will later be deducted from any recording advance or royalties due to the artist.

Many publishers actively promote their assets to use as samples. In the beginning, people in the industry didn't think there was a legitimate market, but now they've heavily sampled all the old catalog titles the publisher owns. Today, publishers are approaching songwriters to send original compositions.

Universal Music Publishing distributes a 2-disc UMG sampler of samples entitled *Great Breaks*. It features snippets of songs such as Rufus's "Sweet Thing" and many other tracks. It is sent to prospective users, including producers and music supervisors.

The newest trend involves producers sampling from movie scores and television theme songs. Jay-Z's huge's hit, "Hard Knock Life," sampled in the Broadway musical *Annie*, opened the door. Likewise for similar covers, such as rap duo Timbaland and Magoo, who used the theme from "Knight Rider," and rapper Busta Rhymes, who used a sample from the '70s hit show *The Six Million Dollar Man*. Artists are now sampling from video games—such as Lil Flip, who sampled the Pacman theme for his *Billboard* hit, "Game Over."

### Transfer of copyrights (assignment)

In most music publishing agreements is a requirement that the songwriter assign the copyright of the written song to the publisher. This is known as a *transfer of copyright* or simply *assignment*. It transfers ownership of the song to the publisher in exchange for the payment to the songwriter of royalties in amounts and time intervals specified in the publishing contract. Typically, song copyrights are held by the music publishers, while sound recordings are controlled by the record companies.

### What is sheet music?

Sheet music is musical notation written on paper—the musical analog of a book. Reading sheet music is the standard way to learn and perform a piece in some cultures and styles of music. In western classical music, it is very rare for a performer to learn a piece in any other way. With the exception of piano, where memorization is expected, classical musicians ordinarily have the sheet music at hand when performing. Even in Jazz, which is mostly improvised, there is a lot of sheet music describing arrangements, melodies, and chord changes.

*Sheet Music* was how the term "publishing" first came to be used in the music business, because it was the right to print (publish) the song on paper. Before you could make recordings or broadcast music on radio, sheet music allowed people to play songs written by other people—usually on the piano in a parlor at home.

Sheet music is less important in other forms of music. In popular music, although sheet music is still produced, nowadays it's more common for people to learn the piece by ear (that is, by imitation). This is also the case in most forms of western folk music. Music of other cultures, both folk and classical, are often transmitted orally, though some have sheet music, and a few use hand signals or some other device as a learning mnemonic.

Sight reading is a musician's ability to perform an unfamiliar work of music upon viewing the sheet music for the first time. Sight reading ability is expected of professional musicians and serious amateurs who play classical music and related forms, especially for church musicians.

### *Why is it called a "mechanical" license?"*

The term mechanical license originated because originally music was mechanically reproduced by mechanical players.

### Who needs sheet music?

Over the years sheet music has become increasingly rare. Generally, there are few instances when sheet music is printed. There used to be a demand for sheet music in cases such as a huge commercial, pop hit record, or a theme song from a hit movie. This is no longer a popular format with the exception of Gospel and Christian music where the sheet music can be helpful in teaching choral parts and arrangements.

### Types of sheet music

Sheet music comes in several different forms. If a piece of music is written for just one instrument (for example, a piano), all the music will be written on just one piece of sheet music. If a piece is intended to be played by more than one person, each person will usually have their own piece of sheet music, called a *part*. If there are a large number of performers required for a piece, there may also be a *score*, which is a piece of sheet music that shows all or most of the instruments' music in one place. Scores come in various forms:

• A *full score* is a large book showing the music of all instruments. It will be large enough for a conductor to use in rehearsals or performance.

• A *miniature score* is like a full score, but reduced in size. It is too small and has too little information for practical use, but handy for studying a piece of music.

• A *study score* is a rather vague term, sometimes used as a synonym for *miniature score*, and sometimes used to mean a score somewhere between the size of a full and a miniature score.

• A ***vocal score*** is a piano score that has all the vocal parts, choral and solo, on separate staves (stanzas or lines). It is used by singers.

A ***short score*** is a reduction of a work for many instruments to just a few staves. Short scores are not usually published, but are often used by composers on their way to producing a finished piece. Often, a short score is completed before work on orchestration begins. *Score* can also refer to the incidental music written for a play, television program, or film (when it is called a film score).

### How a mechanical license works

Mechanical licensing is the licensing of copyrighted musical compositions for use on CDs, records, tapes, and certain digital configurations.

Under the United States Copyright Act, the right to use copyrighted, non-dramatic musical works in the making of phonograph records for distribution to the public for private use is the exclusive right of the copyright owner. However, the copyright act provides that once a copyright owner has recorded and distributed such a work to the U.S. public or permitted another to do so, a compulsory mechanical license is available to anyone else who wants to record and distribute the work in the U.S. upon the payment of license fees at the statutory "compulsory" rate.

### Mechanical license statutory royalty rates

From January 1, 2004, to December 31, 2005, the statutory mechanical royalty rate was:
• 8.50¢ for songs 5 minutes or less
• 1.65¢ per minute or fraction thereof over 5 minutes

### The Harry Fox Agency, Inc.

*operates as an information source, clearing house, and monitoring service for licensing musical copyrights, and acts as a licensing agent for more than 27,000 music publishers, who in turn represent the interests of more than 160,000 songwriters.*

For example:
**Song length x statutory rate = mechanical royalty**
up to 5:00 minutes    8.50¢ (flat rate)   = 8.5¢
5:01—6:00 minutes    1.65¢ x 6 min      = 9.9¢
7:01—8:00 minutes    1.65¢ x 8 min      = 13.2¢

On January 1, 2006, the rate increases to 9.1 cents for songs 5 minutes or less and to 1.75 cents per minute or fraction thereof for songs over 5 minutes. These rates are set by the federal government.

### How do I get a mechanical license?
If you are the record label, you would request it from the music publisher. If you are the music publisher, you create your own mechanical license or hire an agency (such as Harry Fox) to issue it on your behalf.

### Statutory license (compulsory license)
A statutory license confers rights to use content. In the U.S., the terms of usage are defined by the copyright law, as enacted by Congress. Similar laws exist in other countries. For example, radio broadcasters need a license to play music published through ASCAP, BMI, and SESAC. They don't need to obtain permission from the copyright holders to play a song but must pay usage fees to the copyright holders based on how often a particular song is played.

### Controlled composition
A controlled composition is basically a standard discount an artist/writer gives the record company if it agrees to select songs written by the recording artist for the album. The idea is that the artist is "double-dipping"—already getting paid for recording the album—and generating even more income by insisting on using his own songs. So the label asks for a discount on the mechanical royalty they have to pay the artist for the song. These "controlled compositions" reduce the mechanical licensing rate owed by the label to the writer to two-thirds of the statutory rate (which is set by the federal

**To obtain copyright forms** *from the Library of Congress, go to* **www.copyright. gov** *and download PA and SR forms. The registration is $30. You are required to submit an audio copy of your work.*

government). So if the statutory rate is 8.6 cents, the record company only has to pay two-thirds—5.74 cents per song to the artist. This is common practice and is agreed to by both parties in the artist's recording contract.

### The Harry Fox Agency, Inc. (HFA)

Established in 1927, the Harry Fox Agency, a subsidiary of the National Publishers Association, is responsible for issuing and collecting royalties for mechanical licenses on behalf of most U.S. music publishers. For this service, the Harry Fox Agency charges an administration fee of 4.5 percent of the net royalties.

### How does a copyright help me?

A copyright helps prove that you came up with the idea first—a recognized form of ownership.

The Harry Fox Agency can also issue (on behalf of the publisher) a synchronization (sync) license, which is needed when a publisher's music is used in a motion picture, commercial, or on television. The administration fee for the sync license is usually 10 percent of the net royalties, with a maximum of $250 per composition.

HFA licenses the largest percentage of the mechanical and digital uses of music in the United States on CDs, digital services, records, tapes, and imported phonorecords.

The Harry Fox Agency Inc.
711 Third Avenue
New York, NY 10017
www.harryfox.com

### Copyright

A copyright provides its holder (owner) the right to restrict unauthorized copying and reproduction of a literary work, movie, music, painting, software, mask work, etc.). Copyright is used two ways: to mean a form of protection (when you copyright for a song) or the thing that is copyrighted (your song is sometimes referred to as a "copyright," as in: "I own three copyrights").

Copyrights may be granted, sold, or relinquished. Often, a copyright holder will transfer his copyrights to a corporation. For example, a writer who writes a novel will sign a publication agreement with a company such as Random House in which the writer agrees to transfer all copyrights to Random House in exchange for royalties and other terms. One might ask why a copyright holder would ever give up his rights. The answer is that large companies such as Random House have production and marketing capabilities far beyond that of the author. In the digital age of music, it may seem that music may be copied and distributed for a minimal cost through the Internet, but a record label will still provide the great service of promoting and marketing the artist so that his work can reach a much larger audience. A copyright holder does not have to transfer all rights. Some of the rights may be transferred, or the copyright holder may grant another party a non-exclusive license to copy and/or distribute the work in a particular region.

### How to copyright your music

The minute you have completed your creative work and made it into a tangible copy (something you can touch, such as a tape, CD, sheet music, lyrics), under the United States Copyright Law you are the official copyright owner, as long as you can prove the date it was originated. It is advisable to file a copyright form with the Library of Congress, which will legitimize your claim and remain on file with the Library of Congress and remove all doubts concerning such issues as timelines and dates of origination, etc. Even though your work is authorized from the date of origination according to copyright law, it is in your best interest to file a copyright form. If you wish to sell your catalogue or sign a publishing deal at some point, the potential investors would want to see the copyright forms you have filed with the Library of Congress.

**Radio stations pay for the music they play** through performance rights organizations such as BMI, ASCAP, and SESAC.

### The poor man's copyright

Another way to copyright recorded material is to mail a self-addressed, sealed, audible copy of your work to yourself and not open the package upon receiving it in the mail. The fact that the postal seal is binding in a court of law authenticates the date the work was originated. No matter what method you use, once you become the official copyright owner no one can perform your songs *ever* without your getting paid.

### Public domain

Internationally, the public domain is the body of creative works and other knowledge—writing, artwork, music, science, inventions, and others—in which no person or organization has any proprietary interest (as opposed to a government-granted monopoly such as a copyright or patent). Such works and inventions are considered part of the public's cultural heritage, and anyone can use and build upon them without restriction (not taking into account laws concerning safety, export, etc.).

While copyright was created to protect the financial incentive of those doing creative work as a means to encourage more creative work, works in the public domain just exist as such, and the public has the right to use and reuse the creative work of others without financial or social burden.

### Work for hire

According to copyright law, if a work is "made for hire", the employer, and not the employee, is considered the author. The employer may be a firm, an organization, or an individual.

### Copyright collective

A copyright collective or copyright collecting agency is a body created under copyright law that collects royalty payments for copyright holders. The collective may have the authority to license works and collect royalties as part of a statutory scheme or enter into an agreement with the copyright owner to represent the

*All three performance rights organizations (BMI, ASCAP, SESAC) pay pretty much the same …*

*All three pay on different schedules: some quarterly, some biannually, but the end royalty amount is basically the same. Call all three and have them send you a package and see which one works best for you.*

owner's interests when dealing with licensees and potential licensees.

In the U.S. and Canada, when dealing with music, these groups are called performance rights
organizations or PROs.

## Performance Rights Organizations

A **performance rights organization (PRO)** exists to collect and distribute royalties on behalf of audio and video artists, for performances of their copyrighted works under copyright law. In some countries it is called a **copyright collective** or **copyright collecting agency**. A copyright collective is broader than a PRO as it is not limited to performance material.

**BMI**
**Broadcast Music Incorporated**
**www.bmi.com**

BMI is an American performing rights organization that represents approximately 300,000 songwriters, composers, and music publishers in all genres of music. The nonprofit company, founded in 1940, collects license fees on behalf of the American creators it represents, as well as thousands of creators from around the world who choose BMI for representation in the United States. The license fees BMI collects for the public performances of its repertoire of approximately 4.5 million compositions (including radio airplay, broadcast and cable television carriage, Internet, and live and recorded performances, and by all other users of music) are then distributed as royalties to the writers, composers, and copyright holders it represents.

BMI's roster of affiliated songwriters and composers includes outstanding creators in many styles of musical composition: from Pop songwriters to film and television composers; from classical music composers to commercial jingle writers; from library music to musical theater composers; from Jazz to Hip-hop, from Metal to Meringue, from Classical to Classic Soul, from Rock to Reggae.

BMI (New York)
320 West 57th St.
New York, NY 10019
(212) 586-2000 phone
(212) 489-2368 fax

BMI (Los Angeles)
8730 Sunset Boulevard
3rd Floor West
West Hollywood, CA 90069
(310) 659-9109 phone
(310) 657-6947 fax

BMI (Nashville)
10 Music Square East
Nashville, TN 37203
(615) 401-2000 phone
(615) 401-2120 fax

## ASCAP
The American Society of Composers, Authors and Publishers
www.ascap.com

ASCAP is a membership association of over 170,000 U.S. composers, songwriters, lyricists, and music publishers. Through agreements with affiliated international societies, ASCAP also represents hundreds of thousands of music creators worldwide. ASCAP is the only U.S. performing rights organization created and controlled by composers, songwriters, and music publishers, with a board of directors elected by and from the membership.

ASCAP protects the rights of its members by licensing and distributing royalties for the non-

**When music is performed in public . . .** *licensing fees due to the songwriters and publishers are determined and enforced by performance rights organizations.*

dramatic public performances of their copyrighted works. ASCAP's licensees encompass all who want to perform copyrighted music publicly. ASCAP makes giving and obtaining permission to perform music simple for both creators and users of music.

ASCAP (New York)
One Lincoln Plaza
New York, NY 10023
(212) 621-6000 phone
(212) 724-9064 fax

ASCAP (Los Angeles)
7920 Sunset Boulevard, Suite 300
Los Angeles, CA 90046
(323) 883-1000 phone
(323) 883-1049 fax

ASCAP (Nashville)
2 Music Square West
Nashville, TN 37203
(615) 742-5000 phone
(615) 742-5020 fax

**SESAC**
**www.sesac.com**
SESAC, founded in 1930, is the second oldest performing rights organization in the United States. SESAC's repertory, once limited to European and Gospel music, has diversified to include today's most popular music, including dance hits, Rock, Latino, Jazz, Country, and Contemporary Christian music. music.

SESAC (headquarters)
55 Music Square East
Nashville, TN 37203
(615) 320-0055 phone
(615) 329-9627 fax

SESAC– New York
152 West 57th ST
57th Floor
New York, NY 10019
(212) 586-3450 phone · (212) 489-5699 fax

SESAC– Los Angeles, CA
501 Santa Monica Blvd
Suite 450
Santa Monica, CA 90401-2430
(310) 393-9671 phone · (310) 393-6497 fax

SESAC– International
6 Kenrick Place
London W1H 3FF
020 7486 9994 phone · 020 74869929 fax

## What Can a Music Publisher Do for You?

### 1. Administration
Secure copyrights,and pay and collect royalties. The administrator of the copyright will also periodically audit the copyright user.

### 2. Song Plugging
Pitch songs to potential copyright users (producers, record labels, recording artist, and music supervisors).

### 3. Creative Input
Locate or develop relationships with collaborators such as matching a lyricist with a writer who writes only music or tracks.

### 4. Cash Advance
Most music publishers are willing to give their exclusive songwriters substantial cash advances based upon the potential earning value of the copyright rendered under the publishing agreement.

## *Other organizations you need to know about*

### RIAA Recording Industry Association of America
**www.riaa.com**

The RIAA represents the U.S. recording industry. Its mission is to foster a business and legal climate that supports and promotes its members' creative and financial vitality. Its members are the record companies that make up the most vibrant national music industry in the world. RIAA members create, manufacture, and/or distribute approximately 90 percent of all legitimate sound recordings produced and sold in the United States.

MY GOLD RECORD

RIAA works to protect intellectual property rights worldwide and the First Amendment rights of artists; conduct consumer industry and technical research; and monitor and review state and federal laws, regulations and policies. The RIAA also certifies Gold, Platinum, Multi-Platinum, and Diamond sales awards.

### NARAS (The Recording Academy)$^{\Delta}$
### National Association of Recording Arts and Sciences
**www.Grammy.com**

Established in 1957, NARAS is dedicated to improving the quality of life and cultural conditions for music and its makers. NARAS is known worldwide for the Grammy Awards and is responsible for outreach, professional development, cultural enrichment, education, and human services programs.

### NARM
### National Association of  Recording Merchandisers
**www.narm.com**

NARM is a not-for-profit trade association founded in 1958. Its nearly 1,000 member companies represent the retailers, wholesalers, and distributors of prerecorded music in the U.S. Members include such familiar retailing names as Tower, Best Buy (which includes Musicland, Sam Goody), Wherehouse, TransWorld Entertainment (which includes Camelot, Coconuts, Record Town, Specs, Strawberries, The Wall, Waxie Maxie, FYE), Borders Books and Music, Target, Newbury Comics, Waterloo Records, CDNow, and Amazon.com.

NARM's associate member companies represent the full spectrum of entertainment suppliers including major record labels, independent labels, home video companies, as well as companies offering products and services which support entertainment retailing. Associate members include such companies as Arista, Capitol, Epic, RCA, Warner Bros., MCA, Rounder, Telarc, Walt Disney, Welk Music Group, Wind-Up, Paramount Home Video, Buena Vista, Case Logic, Recoton, and *Billboard* magazine.

NARM's mission is to represent the common interests of its members to industry and public policy makers and to promote the visibility and image of the entertainment software industry.

*NARM conventions are where music retailers of all sizes— from mom & pop stores all the way to huge chains—discuss ways to expand their business and come up with solutions for common problems. It's the one convention where record label executives and store owners can sit down together to exchange ideas for advertising and special in-store promotions for the coming year.*

### AFIM
### Association for Independent Music
### www.afim.org
AFIM is the voice of the independent music industry. Founded in 1972, it is a professional trade organization dedicated to insuring the vitality of the independent music industry. AFIM's mission is to create business opportunities for its members through an annual convention, and through ongoing information services and educational resource materials. AFIM is also an advocacy group, speaking out on the issues most relevant to its membership.

**MIDEM**

**www.midem.com**

MIDEM (short for *Marché international de l'Èdition musicale*) is the world's largest music industry trade fair, which is held annually at the Palais des Festivals in France. Bringing together musicians, business people, cultural policy makers, and journalists from many countries, it provides a forum for business talks, discussing political and legal issues, and showcasing new artists, musical trends, and music-related products.

## How a Copyright Works

The copyright code of the United States (title 17 of the U.S. Code) provides for copyright protection in sound recordings. Sound recordings are defined as "works that result from the fixation of a series of musical, spoken, or other sounds, but not including the sounds accompanying a motion picture or other audiovisual work." Common examples include recordings of music, drama, or lectures.

Copyright in a sound recording protects the specific series of sounds "fixed" (embodied in a recording) against unauthorized reproduction and revision, unauthorized distribution of phonorecords containing those sounds, and certain unauthorized performances by means of a digital audio transmission. The Digital Performance Right in Sound Recordings Act of 1995, P.L. 104-39, effective February 1, 1996, created a new limited performance right for certain digital transmissions of sound recordings.

Several things can be copyrighted in any sound recording of a song. There are the actual sounds—the performance of the work. And there are the notes the musicians play to create the song—which could be embedded in sheet music. There are the lyrics for the song—they can be written down on a sheet of paper. According to the the U.S. copyright office, copyright protection extends to the contribution of the performer(s) whose performance is captured.

*Magazine advertisement from the early 20th Century*

# SAMPLE CLEARANCE FORM

### 1. New Work
- The title of the new work
- The full name of the writer(s) and publisher information for the new work including affiliation:
- The name of the record company planning to release the new work
- Projected release date and release number
- The artist's name:
- Record label and address:
- Label number (if available):
- Album title:
- Singles, remixes, etc. planned for release:
- A copy of the new lyrics
- A high quality audio copy containing the original composition, and the new work containing the sample/interpolation. If possible, also include the sample excerpt(s)
- Acceptable audio audio formats: DAT, Compact Disc. Audio cassette may also be used however, it MUST be a high quality recording.

### 2. Original Work
- Title of original work:
- Original artist:
- Brief description of original work within new work:

All sample requests must be accompanied by a recording of the new work, no exceptions.

### Sample Clearance Form
### 1. New Work

Artist: _____

Title of new work work: _____

Does it contain any other samples?(which): _____
_____
_____

The full name of each of the writer(s) for the new work including affiliation:
_____
_____
_____

Record label and address: _____
_____
_____

Label number (if available): _____

Album title:_____

Singles, remixes, etc. planned for release:_____

_____

_____

Initial pressing (number of copies):_____

Distribution: _____

Proposed release date: _____

## 2. Original Work

Title of original work:_____

Original artist:_____

Brief description of original work within new work: _____

_____

_____

_____

## 3. Any further information we may find useful

_____

_____

_____

_____

_____

_____

_____

_____

_____

_____

_____

**Contact Information: Date:_____/_____/_____**

Company:_____

Contact:_____

Address

1:_____

Address

2:_____

City:_____ State:_____ Postal Code: _____

Phone Number:_____ Fax Number:_____

Email Address: _____

# How Music Ge

*A recorded track is made of two components that gen*

| | Who owns it? | What royalties are earne |
|---|---|---|
| **THE SONG**  The idea for a performance. It includes words and music, which can be described on paper and protected with a copyright. | **Songwriter (50%)** → 50% to writer of music. 50% to writer of words. <br><br> **Publisher (50%)**   Co-publishing deal: publisher and songwriter and other parties may split publishing share. | **Performance royalties** ——— are earned every time a song is played on the radio or TV or performed live. <br><br> **Mechanical royalties** ——— are paid on every copy of the song that is sold on CDs manu- factured by the record company. |
| **THE RECORDED PERFORMANCE**  The song as interpreted and recorded by artists, musicians, and producers. Can be manufacturer and sold to consumers, licensed to movies and television, and broadcast on radio. | **The record company** usually owns the master recording in perpetuity (forever) and pays royalties to the artist as it earns income from the recording. Occasionally ownership reverts back to the recording artist, or is shared with the artist, after the recording costs have been paid back. <br><br> Recorded performances also earn royalties for artists when they are used in movies, appear on movie soundtracks, TV commercials, ring tones, video games, and as samples in other artists' recordings. | **Artist royalties** are earned on ——— every copy sold. The artist will be paid after recording and other costs have been deducted (recouped) from royalties earned. <br><br> **Producer royalties** are earned on every copy sold. The producer will be paid after recording and other costs have been deducted from royalties earned. <br><br> **Sync license fees** are paid when songs are put in movies, TV shows, commercials, etc., usually a flat, negotiated fee. <br><br> Royalties are paid for masters used on soundtrack albums. |

# ates Royalties

*ne: The song and the performance (master recording)*

| Who collects the royalties ? | How much can you earn? |
|---|---|
| ·ry Fox Agency in most cases %) is hired by the artist to collect · money and make sure that the culations are correct. Fox agency ·es a percentage as commission. → | From January 1, 2004, to December 31, 2005: 8.50¢ for songs 5 minutes or less OR, for songs over 5 minutes, 1.65¢ per minute or fraction thereof for every copy sold. For a five-minute or shorter track on a million-selling album, the amount would be $85,000. Starting in 2006, the rate increases to 9.1¢ for a five-minute song, which would amount to $91,000 on a million-selling album. |
| ·ormance rights organizations :AP, BMI, and SESAC). → | For a typical Billboard "Hot 100" No. 1 song, revenue should be around a million dollars, give or take a couple hundred thousand dollars. |
| ·lly the artist's manager or ·ness manager collects. ·agement usually takes 10–15 ·ent off the top, before other ·nses are deducted. → | For an artist, a negotiated royalty is paid anywhere from 8 percent to 12 percent. Before the artist receives any royalties, album costs such as the artist advance, recording cost, marketing, promotion, and video cost must be recouped by the record company from the royalties.

The producer usually receives a royalty between 2 and 5 percent, but before any royalties are paid to him, the cost of recording and his advance are recouped. |

# 5.

·················

# Songwriting and Song Placement

Songwriting is an age-old craft that's become a lucrative industry in itself. A successful commercial hit can bring in millions of dollars in royalties for the songwriter or copyright owner. After a songwriter has written a song, he or she usually creates a demonstration version with a specific artist in mind, and begins the tedious process of trying to get the song recorded by the prospective artist. This is known as song placement and is very difficult if you don't know the artist, the artist's manager, or an A&R executive at the record label.

### Artist and Repertoire (A&R)

A&R is the division of a label responsible for scouting and developing talent. The A&R department is the link between the recording artist/act and the record label, and often handles finding acts, negotiating contracts, and scheduling recording sessions.

One of the A&R department's main jobs is sorting through demo tapes sent to the label by hopefuls. A&R departments typically only accept demos they solicit, or those from familiar business contacts.

If you are not affiliated with a major music publisher, you must first make sure your material is copyrighted and find out if the artist or the artist's manager or label accepts unsolicited material. Even if they accept it, it's a long shot to get the song placed with the artist.

To pursue the "unsolicited material" approach, try and establish contact with A&R execs, set up meetings with them, and be persistent. Remember

## Digital Songwriting Tools

*Can't translate your songs into music notation? Let your computer do it. Two major players in music notation software are:*

**Sibelius**—*claiming to be the world's best-selling music notation software for Windows and Mac, the program is as intuitive to use as a pen, yet so powerful that it does most things quicker than the blink of an eye. www.sibelius.com*

**Finale 2005** *provides simpler, richer and more intuitive interaction for unsurpassable results in creating, customizing and sharing printed music. www.finalemusic.com*

that they are paid to find great songs and, even though they may not respond immediately, your persistence may pay off.

Check out and participate in songwriting contests or songwriting showcases. Consult your performance rights organizations, ASCAP and BMI. They often hold writer workshops, which can be very effective for learning good songwriting techniques, making valuable contacts, and networking.

### Copyright notice
The copyright notice includes the copyright symbol and/or word, the year, and name of copyright owner: © 2006 Your Company Name.

A principle of U.S. law is that an author of a work may reap the fruits of his or her intellectual creativity for a limited period of time. Copyright is a form of protection provided by the U.S. laws governing original works of authorship, including literary, dramatic, musical, architectural, cartographic, choreographic, pantomimic, pictorial, graphic, sculptural, and audiovisual creations.

"Copyright" literally means the right to copy. The term has come to mean the body of exclusive rights

Nº 17. Hunters Chorus from „THE ROSE OF ERIN."

Published by JOHN F. STRATTON, New.York.

### What is a musical score?

An orchestra conductor needs to see all the instrumental parts at the same time. Above, you can see what each of the 12 instruments is playing for the first 12 bars of a song from the United States Civil War.

granted by law to authors for protection of their work. The copyright owner has the exclusive right to reproduce, distribute, and, in the case of certain works, publicly perform or display the work; to prepare derivative works; in the case of sound recordings, to perform the work publicly by means of a digital audio transmission; and to license others to engage in the same acts under specific terms and conditions.

Copyright protection does not extend to any idea, procedure, process, slogan, principle, or discovery.

### Musical score

A musical score is a blueprint of a musical work that shows all musical parts (violins, horns, vocals, etc.) on the same page. For example, at the top of the page may be the vocal part, followed by the piano portion, followed by the horns, etc. With so much information on each page of the score, perhaps only four measures will fit on a page, so scores usually have many pages.

### Writer breakdown (percentages)

Writer breakdown is a list that shows who owns which songs and how the publishing rights and revenue are split—the writers' and publishers' share of songs on an album or single. The writer breakdown also specifies the amount that each writer will receive and the percentage that the publishers receive. For example, the producer and the writer may contribute 50 percent music and 50 percent melody; in most cases producers only do music. In a co-publishing agreement, the breakdown specifies who owns what, and who wrote what; this information determines the royalty information.

If the producer hires a separate lyricist (lyric writer) the producer and the writer usually split the ownership of the copyright equally: 50 percent of the music and 50 percent of the melody, although in most cases producers only write the music. If a lyricist is involved, the typical split is still 50 percent of the revenues for the copyright owners. The music itself, more commonly referred to as the track, is also considered as 50 percent. If the melody is separate from the lyrics, the melody portion is further split into 25 percent melody and 25 percent lyrics. In other words, the lyricist would receive 25 percent of the total writer's royalties. These splits are specified and agreed to in the writer's agreement and in the co-publishing agreement. When the songs are copyrighted, these splits are described in the legal paperwork.

The information is then written up as a **co-publishing agreement**, which shows how the writing and publishing royalties will be divided and paid. The agreement is signed by all writing and publishing parties involved.

### Composer

A composer is one who writes music. The term refers particularly to someone who writes music in some type of musical notation, thus allowing others to perform the music. This distinguishes the composer from a musician who improvises. However, a person may be called a composer without creating music in written form, since not all musical genres rely on written notation. In this context, the composer is the originator of the music, and usually its first performer. Later performers then repeat the musical composition they have heard.

The term "composer" is often used specifically to mean a composer in the Western tradition of classical music. In popular and folk music, the composer is called a songwriter, since the music generally takes the form of a song.

## Different Styles of Songwriting

**Rhythm and Blues** or **R&B**, is a musical marketing term introduced in the late 1940s by *Billboard* to replace the term "race music," which was considered offensive. Rather than describing a recognizable musical genre, *rhythm and blues* has come to be used to indicate whatever contemporary music is popular with African Americans.

**Hip-hop** is a cultural movement that began among urban (primarily, but not entirely, African American) youth in New York and has spread around the world. The four main elements of Hip-hop are MCing, DJing, graffiti artistry, and breakdancing. The term has since come to be a synonym for rap music to mainstream audiences. The two are not, however, interchangeable: Rapping (MCing) is the vocal expression of lyrics in sync to a rhythm beneath it.

**Pop**—depending on the context—is either an abbreviation of popular music or a term for a sub-genre of it. The subgenre of pop is perhaps the

## What does the copyist do?

*The copyist takes the full music score, as written out by the composer, and copies all the separate parts for each of the musicians. After all, only the composer needs to see all the parts at once. The musicians just need to know their individual parts. They count throughout the entire performance to make sure they start and stop playing on time.*

most widely crowd-pleasing form of popular music. As a rule, pop music features simple, memorable melodies with catchy, singalong choruses, and instrumentally features heavy use of synthesizer backing. It is instantly accessible to anyone culturally initiated, even the musically inept. Successful pop music (which is usually measured in terms of its commercial success without any pretense to broader artistic goals) is usually performed by charismatic performers who may or may not be musically talented, but who look attractive and may dance well. Songwriting and arranging may be performed by anonymous but well-paid sound producers.

*Jazz*, a musical form that grew out of a cross-fertilization of Folk Blues, Ragtime, and European music—particularly band music—has been called the first art form to develop in the U.S.

*Gospel* combines Christian religious lyrics with melody and rhythm that developed in tandem with early Blues and Jazz. Modern Gospel artists have also incorporated elements from Soul music, which originally arose as a secular form of Gospel. Gospel music first grew popular with African Americans and white southerners but has since become popular around the world.

*Classical music* is a broad, somewhat imprecise term, referring to music rooted in the traditions of European art, ecclesiastical and concert music, particularly between 1000 and 1900. This tradition developed between 1550 and 1825, centering on what is known as the common practice period.

*Melody* is a series of notes played in succession, not simultaneously as in a chord. However, this succession must be perceived as an single entity to be called a melody. The main theme of a work is often called the melody. It consists of one or more musical phrases, and is usually repeated throughout a song or piece in various forms.

**Lyrics** refer to the words of a song. They are usually written during or after the underlying music is composed. However, it is possible that music is added after the lyrics are written. A person who specializes in writing words for music is a *lyricist*.

**Songwriter** is a person who writes the music for songs. "Songwriter" also implies that the same person has written the lyrics, although this is not always the case. Songwriters may sing the songs they write, or may write songs for others to sing. People who sing their own songs are often called *singer-songwriters*.

**Singer-songwriter** refers to a performer who both writes and sings her own material. This distinguishes her from artists who are only singers.

**Film score** is the background music in a film, usually specifically written for the film and often used to heighten emotions provoked by the imagery on the screen or by the dialogue. In some cases, film themes have become accepted as classical music.

A **film composer** is usually contacted after the film has been shot. He is shown an unpolished "rough cut" of the film, and talks to the director about what sort of music should be used. He will then work on creating this music. When the music has been composed and orchestrated, it is then performed by the orchestra or ensemble, often with the composer conducting. The orchestra performs in front of a large screen showing the movie, and sometimes a "click track" is used—a series of clicks that help the conductor synchronize the orchestra's playing to the film's action.

**Soundtrack** is a compilation of songs either inspired by or including portions of a film's music. A soundtrack typically includes contributions from a single artist or various artists. Over the last few decades, movie soundtracks have become some of the best sellers in music history, such as *The Bodyguard* and *Saturday Night Fever*.

**The metronome** *is still used today to tap out a constant beat for musicians to keep time as they practice. You simply wind it up, set the speed, and let it click: no electricity or electronics is involved. In recording studios the metronome has been replaced by a click track, which is played through the conductor's headphones.*

One way to record a soundtrack
is to assemble an orchestra on
a soundstage where the movie
sequence can be seen on a screen
by the conductor (see the screen
behind orchestra above).
The conductor then directs
the orchestra to play in time
with the action.

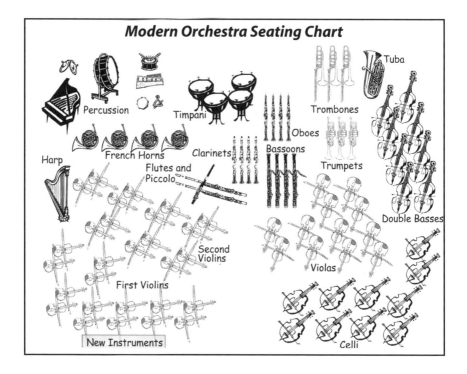

# 6.

. . . . . . . . . . . . . .

# Marketing & Promotion

Next to creating a great product, marketing and promotion are the most important aspects of selling a record. If consumers are never made aware of the product (whether good or bad), how can they decide whether or not to purchase it? For that reason, marketing and promotion are essential to selling any product. In this chapter we cover marketing and promotion as it relates to retail (stores), print and media, street level, word-of-mouth, and direct to the consumer.

## The Basics

### Marketing budget
The marketing budget is the amount of money allocated for marketing of a recording project or single recording, based on the marketing plan. The marketing budget is earmarked for retail programs, such as listening stations, sales pricing, retail displays, monthly mailers, magazines, radio ads, etc.

### Promotion budget
A promotion budget is money used to increase the sales of product. The budget may be spent on video, radio, independent promotion, tastemakers, listening parties, DJ parties, etc.

### Demographics
The term demographics refers to selected characteristics of a population (age and income distribution and trends, mobility, educational attainment, home ownership and employment status, for instance) for purposes of marketing, marketing

## What's in a marketing plan?

*A marketing plan details the actions necessary to achieve specific marketing goals within a specific budget. On a baby act, for example, a label may spend $50,000 on marketing and promotion —not much, in other words . So making every penny count is crucial. How can you get the most bang for your buck so that label may be willing to add more money to the budget? Do you:*

**a** *Spend it all on a cheap video?*

**b** *Try to get on celebrity mix tapes?*

**c** *Try to get on mix shows?*

**d** *Service record pools?*

**e** *Do a few things but only in a certain geographical area?*

**See marketing plan example on the last five pages of this chapter**

## What's in an EPK?

*An EPK (electronic press kit) includes digital information on a DVD or CD (movies, music samples, press clippings, scanned photos, reviews, tour information) plus footage of the artist being interviewed and performing. And EPK is usually sent out with printed information or anything else that spurs interest. EPKs and press kits are instrumental in securing TV appearances by showing producers how artists interact with hosts and appear on camera.*

*EPKs are sent to retail buyers, concert promoters, and tastemakers—i.e. those who can help artist get employment, sponsorships, and funding.*

research, opinion research, and the study of consumer behavior. Marketers often group consumers into segments based on demographic variables. These market segments are sometimes referred to as "demographics". That is, a marketer might speak of the single, female, middle-class, age 18 to 24 demographic.

### Publicists and public relations(PR) firms

Publicists are responsible for getting information about the artist to the public, whether by radio and television interviews or through the print media. The efforts of the publicist or public relations firm are invaluable. The publicist's job is to inform or influence specific publications using writing, marketing, advertising, publicity, promotions, and special events. Some publicists work as full-time employees of record companies, artists, or producers; others work for PR agencies that contract their services to clients that pay for their expertise at keeping them in or out of the spotlight, whichever is necessary.

### Press release

A press release is a written or recorded communication directed at members of the news media for the purpose of announcing something of news value. Typically, it is mailed or faxed to assignment editors at newspapers, magazines, radio stations, television stations, and networks.

### Album review

A rating system published by a trade or consumer magazine, newspaper, or television show that can influence your listening audience. A good album review can increase sales and help start a "buzz."

### Press kit

A press kit is a packaged set of promotional materials of a recording artist represented for promotional use. The kit will usually include a CD or advance copy along with reviews, photos, and background information on the person, band, or group and is distributed for publicity reasons among media sources like radio stations. They are often distributed to announce a release or for a news conference.

## Promotion

### Tour support

Tour support is the money that's allocated to support a new recording artist in the beginning of their touring career, especially when there's no audience demand for the artist on the touring circuits. In other words, promoters are not willing to spend money on artists that consumers won't recognize or pay to see. But record companies understand the importance of touring and getting an artist in front of as many potential buyers as possible in the hopes that performances in various venues will cause a "buzz" and eventually drive the consumer to record retailers.

Touring also gives the publicity and promotional departments an opportunity to coordinate their efforts with the touring schedule and to book the artist on radio and TV interviews, as well as coordinating in-store events with the artist in various markets where performances take place. The record company views this as an investment in promoting the album and eventually they hope to see a return on their investment. In the past, this was solely the expense of the record company, but today the record company may expect to recoup its investment from the artist directly from the artist's royalties.

### When should I hire a publicist?

*It is wise to to retain the services of a publicist 90 to 120 days before a project is released, since most magazines and TV shows edit the content 90-120 days before air or publication date. Most publicists require a monthly retainer, usually between $2,000 and $5,000+ per month, plus expenses.*

### Promotional dates

Promotional dates are artist performances or appearances that are exclusively for the purpose of promoting the artist's album. The artist is usually obligated by contract to do a number of these appearances on behalf of the record company,

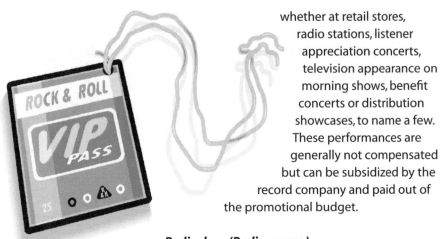

whether at retail stores, radio stations, listener appreciation concerts, television appearance on morning shows, benefit concerts or distribution showcases, to name a few. These performances are generally not compensated but can be subsidized by the record company and paid out of the promotional budget.

### Radio drop (Radio promo)

Recording artists can be helpful to radio stations by going in a studio—their personal studios or label studios or a radio station studio—and recording greetings that the radio stations can play to introduce their songs or various radio station events— such as: "Hi, this is Beyoncé, and you're listening to NightBeat..."

## *Retail*

### Positioning

In music marketing, positioning is the technique of creating an image or identity for a product or an artist. It is the *place* a product occupies in a given market as perceived by the target market, via listening stations, special sales during Black Music Month, and special buyer incentives like getting a discount on a particular artist's previous albums if you purchase their new release.

### SoundScan

SoundScan is an electronic network that collects weekly retail figures from over 17,000 music stores in the U.S., including chains such as Tower, Wherehouse, and Best Buy. Soundscan is owned and operated by a company based in White Plains, New York: VNU Marketing Information. VNU sells their information to corporate subscribers like record labels and concert promoters for lots of money. Since 1991, *Billboard* charts have been based on SoundScan data.

How does SoundScan scan all those sounds? Barcodes. Subscribers can track sales for artists in particular regions, compare sales figures within genres, and monitor the efficacy of the tiniest indie promotional effort or the biggest Britney blowout. VNU also offers BookScan and VideoScan services.

The switch to SoundScan data more than a decade ago drastically altered the *Billboard* charts. Before, the charts had been compiled from dubious data delivered by radio stations and record stores. Now, SoundScan provides an uncompromising retail x-ray of music-buying in America.

### Listening station

Listening stations are the electronic devices that you see in most major retail stores that feature the new releases and sometimes a brief bio of the featured recording artist, along with a listing of the featured album's tracks. Listening stations are marketing opportunities purchased by the album's distributor directly from the retail account. On the national chain level this is usually done through the corporate office and is sold as a national campaign, which means that all stores across the nation will feature the exact same presentation of product.

### What is a bullet?

Bullet is a term used in music industry trade charts to describe a charted record that is increasing its momentum as it rises up the charts. In other words, a "number one with a bullet" means that the top seller is still gaining momentum—not losing it. A number without a bullet means that the record has either maintained its sales rate or has dropped below.

### Retail sales programs

*…such as listening stations and special sale pricing are generally paid for out of the marketing co-op budget and are viewed by the record company as opportunities to get more product into the stores. The process works the same at regional and even Mom and Pop accounts. Generally, a label's regional sales rep works out the terms of a price & positioning sales program with the store's music buyer.*

### In-store (event)

An in-store event is a scheduled promotional appearance by an artist in a particular retail store or outlet where the artist makes him or herself available to customers for autograph signings and giveaways of promotional items. The event is usually coordinated by the record company, the distributor's regional sales representative, or by the promotional representative. When an artist is slated to appear in a particular market, the record label and its distributor coordinate their efforts to make sure the artist visits the key retail accounts, who always appreciate it when the artist comes in personally and interacts with the fans. The retailer will usually give away flyers and sponsor radio ads announcing that an artist will be in the store on a certain date, all in the hopes of bringing customers into the stores. The record companies target different retail accounts and usually prefer the ones that report the largest amount of product selling in that region.

### Guaranteed buy-in

If a distributor agrees to participate in a listening station retail program, for example, the retail account agrees to purchase a specific number of pieces of that particular product, which guarantees the distributor a designated amount of product in each of the retailer's individual stores as well as shelf space. Statistics show that listening stations greatly improve the sales by allowing the consumer to hear the music before buying it. It is a win-win situation for the retailer and distributor because the money exchanged for purchasing the program offsets the wholesale price to the retail account, which reduces the cost of the per unit to the retailers.  Example: if the distributor is paying $8.50 per unit wholesale and the retail program brings  him $1.10 per unit, the distributor is now reducing his per unit cost to $7.40.

### Free goods (promotional product)

Free goods is a term used to describe pieces of product that will not be sold but will be made available for promotional purposes. Usually, it is stamped "to be used for promotional purposes only." The bar code is removed so it cannot be scanned.

**PROMOTIONAL USE ONLY**
NOT FOR SALE

### Parental advisory

A parental advisory is a notice to consumers that recordings identified by this logo may contain strong language or depictions of violence, sex, or substance abuse, and that parental discretion is advised. The label is a non-removable logo that record companies voluntarily place on products to better inform consumers and retailers while also protecting the rights of artists. The decision to label a particular sound recording is made by each record company in conjunction with the artist. The industry as a whole and its individual companies take this program seriously. Virtually every sound recording to come under public scrutiny has featured a parental advisory label. The fact is, these recordings account for a fraction of the music being produced. For example, in an average record retail store with 110,000 individual album titles, approximately 500 might carry the Parental Advisory label. That's less than half of one percent of the store's total inventory.

**PARENTAL ADVISORY**
**EXPLICIT CONTENT**

The parental advisory affects the marketing of an album because certain stores—such as Walmart—will not carry titles with this logo. You may have to make an edited version to get into these outlets.

### Trade publications ("trades")

Music industry "trades" show market trends, what radio stations around the country are currently playing, what's hot and what's not. They also keep you abreast of market trends, which records are breaking in particular regions of the country, and they also gauge the airplay activity of a record (how much it's getting

played). Record labels trust and depend on this data to determine where to commit their marketing dollars. Some of the leading trades include:

**Hits**
14958 Ventura Blvd.
Sherman Oaks, CA 91403
(818) 501-7900

**Radio and Records**
10100 Santa Monica Blvd., 5th floor
Los Angeles, CA 90067-4004
(310) 553-4330

**Billboard**
1515 Broadway
New York, NY 10036-8986
(212) 764-7300

*Billboard*—founded in 1894—originally covered carnival entertainment. But as music coverage grew, other subjects were spun off into a separate journal in the 1950s. On January 4, 1936, *Billboard* published its first music hit parade, and on July 20, 1940, it published its first "Music Popularity Chart."

Today, it maintains several international pop charts that track the most popular songs in various categories on a weekly basis. Its "Hot 100" survey ranks the top 100 pop songs and is frequently used as the standard measure for ranking singles in the United States. The "Hot 100" chart is compiled by tracking singles sales and radio airplay on various station formats, including Urban, Modern Rock, Country, Adult Contemporary, Top 40, Rhythmic, and Adult Top 40. Because few musicians release singles in America today, *Billboard* weights a song's radio play as 80 percent and its singles sales as 20 percent to calculate the weekly "Hot 100" rankings.

Since late 1998, it has been possible for a song to chart on the "Hot 100" based only on airplay points (the term *Billboard* uses for this is "album cut"). Previously, a song needed to become a commercial single (available for purchase) in order to rank on the "Hot 100." To date, several songs that were never released as commercial singles have managed to achieve such massive radio airplay that they were able to make it into the No. 1 spot. The first instance was Aaliyah's "Try Again" from *Romeo Must Die*, which was a giant Pop, Rhythmic, and Urban radio hit.

Some other notable *Billboard* world records include Mariah Carey and Boyz II Men's 1995 song, "One Sweet Day," which is the longest-lasting No. 1 on the "Hot 100" (16 weeks) and consequently the most popular song in American history.

### Music conferences

Music business conferences are a great place to introduce and promote new or established artists. Conferences are attended by music business heavyweights and allow personal access to some of the industry's most powerful people. Most conventions contain new artist showcases where they perform and display their talents and also allow you participate. Remember, it was at a music business convention where the multi-platinum rapper $MASE$ first met the president of his future record label: Sean "Puffy" Combs.

*Popular music conferences you can attend*
Visit these Websites for detailed information.
**www.billboard.com**
**www.cmj.com**
**www.midwestmusic summit.com**
**www.gopmc.com**
**www.midem.com**
**www.gospelmusic.org**
**www.gmwa.org**
**www.rronline.com**

## *Music Video and Direct-to-Consumer*

### Music video
A music video or video clip is a short film meant to present a visual representation of a song.

### Video treatment
A short written description of a story intended to be turned into a music video. It may include details of directorial style. Treatments are widely used within the music video industry as selling documents.

### Video commissioner
An employee of the record label responsible for soliciting and hiring video directors and production companies to create music videos.

### Video promoter
A video promoter is hired by the record company to promote a music video to the appropriate outlets.

### Video budget
The money allocated for the production and marketing of a music video. The budget can be a "standalone" or a "promotion" budget. The cost of the music video is usually recouped from the artist's royalties.

### BET (Black Entertainment Television)
BET is the first television network geared toward African Americans. It airs several popular music programs such as 106 & Park and Rap City Midnite Love. BET was founded in 1980 by Robert L. Johnson, who is the chairman and chief executive officer. Today, BET is owned by Viacom.

### MTV
MTV is a cable television network originally devoted to popular rock and other music videos. It later became an outlet for a variety of programs for adolescents and young adults.

### VH1

VH1 (Video Hits 1) is an American cable television channel that was created in 1985. With then four-year-old MTV's popularity rising drastically among teens, VH1 began with the intention to capitalize ⟨ success of the music video. However, VH1's ⟨ to focus on the lighter, softer side of popula including such musicians as Elton John, Stir Diana Ross, Billy Joel, Kenny G, and Anita Baker, to appeal to listeners between 18 and 35+.

### Record pools

Record pools are membership organizations for disk jockeys. Members pay dues to the pool, usually a sm annual fee of less than $1,000. In exchange, receive new record releases from many labels, which otherwise would be very expensive to purchase. Record pools track a variety of information, such as how often a record is played and audience reaction it elicits. The information is passed on to the record companies. Record pools are an effective way to start a buzz and get into the club circuit. The information record pools gather from members is used to compile *Billboard*'s dance charts, since club play is a part of the dance charts formula. Pools can be essential to breaking dance chart records and breaking them early.

## Street Level

### Street team

A relatively new concept in the record business, street teams came into the forefront within the last two decades. Teams promote product or events by tacking up posters, snipes, flyers etc., on abandoned buildings, construction sites, telephone poles, and street lamps. They may hand out T-shirts, postcards, and flyers at concerts, clubs, and college campuses to potential record buyers. Street teams are effective in densely populated urban areas and are hired by the record company or the artist's management team.

### Mixtapes

Mixtapes are the number one source for hot Hip-hop tracks, remixes, blends, live tracks, special mixes, interviews, and fresh new music. Mixtape DJs constantly create and move mixtapes so mixtapes stay current. Mixtapes occupy a gray area in the music industry. Unlike a compilation, which is officially put out by a record company, a mixtape respects no intellectual property laws. Also known as "party tapes," mixtapes usually consist of a recordings of club performances and are intended to be sold by street vendors, the corner record store, and at swap meets. In the 1970s, the Soulsonic Force and others would often distribute recordings of their club performances via audio cassette, as well as customized recordings. However, with artists often giving material to DJs expressly to use on a mixtape, there is not much a record label could do, or would want to do. The mixtape can act as a flyer for the record company's artist, getting a sample of the work to a desirable audience that can make or break underground artists.

# MARKETING PLAN EXAMPLE

| Artist | Album | |
| --- | --- | --- |
| Street date: | | |
| Single selections | Writer/producer | Add date |
| 1. | | |
| 2. | | |

**TARGET MARKETS:** New York, Los Angeles, Philadelphia, Chicago, Washington, DC.

## RADIO

After the single is serviced, all DJs will receive album promotional materials to increase awareness and encourage support.

## RETAIL

Retail reps will provide POP (Point of Purchase display materials) in target markets and work with radio to promote in-store appearances while artist is on promotional visits.

## PUBLICITY

Create cost-effective teaser campaign with weekly reminders by e-cards and fax blitzes.

## PRINT

Advertisements in select media outlets in target markets.

## TELEVISION

Regional BET ads late night Friday and Saturday.

## INTERNET

Banner/snippet campaign tied to chat times and new artist-featured stories.

## GRASS ROOTS

• Marketing that directly targets and touches people where they live, work, entertain, and party.
• Focus on areas with street team promotions in college areas, nightlife areas, concerts, and P.O.P., to ensure promotional product is delivered and serviced timely for daily and key events.
• Events include in-stores, pre-release parties, grand openings, concerts, and

**MARKETING PLAN EXAMPLE**

other youth-related activities.
• Street promoters will also interface with the youth in the faith community to provide promotional product to church youth events and activities.

**PRE-RELEASE**
• Key press
• Key music conferences including NARM
• Street team to distribute postcards, P.O.P., T-Shirts
• Marketing materials distribution
• Press release of signing to record label
• Single release to radio
• Street team paraphernalia distribution in target markets
• Internet promotion with chat times and give-aways
• Pre-sale campaign planned with distributor
• Artist to visit key media, radio, retail, and church events in target markets.

**SALES AND RETAIL**
Independent national account promotions provided by X Promotions for additional retail support and sales tracking in key one-stops and Mom & Pop stores.

| Markets | Retail Outlet |
| --- | --- |
| Los Angeles | Wherehouse |
| New York | Virgin |
| Philadelphia | City Sound |
| Chicago | George's Music Room |

**ADVERTISING SCHEDULE**

|  | Jan | Feb | Mar | Apr | May | Jun | July |
| --- | --- | --- | --- | --- | --- | --- | --- |
| MusicPlus.com | X | | | | | | |
| LoudMusic.com | X | | | | | | |
| Radio | X | | | | | | |
| Billboard | | | X | | | | |
| Urban Inspired | | X | | | | | |

**INTERNET PROMOTION**
• e-Card campaign to begin one week prior to single release date and to continue throughout campaign.

| Interactive e-Card: | www.website.com | www.website.com |
| --- | --- | --- |
| www.website.com | www.website.com | www.website.com |

## MARKETING PLAN EXAMPLE

- Create an enhanced group Website

| | |
|---|---|
| Downloadable bio | Downloadable pictures |
| Sample of single snippits | Links to above websites |
| Tour dates | Banner ads |
| On-line chat hours with "Urban" topics | |

**MERCHANDISING**

All merchandising will reemphasize the marketing message. We will utilize highly visual packaging and design that will highlight the youth movement and music experience.

| | |
|---|---|
| Postcards: 4x8 Glossy | Fax sheets: 8x10 |
| Posters 24x36, street team to service | Flats, endcaps |
|    to key radio and retail, barber shops, | T-shirts |
|    hair salons, etc. | In-store video loops |
| One-sheet | |

**RADIO PROMOTION**

Radio and consistent appearances in target markets are the driving forces behind a single's growth and popularity.

**SET UP**
**First Single:**

Ships to radio: July 01, 2006
Radio add date: July 8, 2006
Marketing campaign countdown to street date (TBD)
Internet banner ads and chat times
Radio promotions tie-in with retail and Internet sites
Promo ads

| Target Markets: | Radio Station |
|---|---|
| New York | WBLS |
| Los Angeles | KJLH |
| Philadelphia | WDAS |
| Washington, DC | WHUR |
| Atlanta | WVEE |
| Chicago | WGCI |

## MARKETING PLAN EXAMPLE

**PUBLICITY**
• PR campaign will begin with the release of the group's signing to the record label and distribution deal
• Internet banner ads will be posted on all key Websites.
• E-cards will be sent to all key outlets weekly, announcing the radio release and record release.
• Press releases and story pitches will be serviced to all key media to secure featured stories, CD reviews and/or mentions.
• Panel discussion and performance pitching.

| Publications | Type | Circulation |
|---|---|---|
| Vibe magazine | Monthly | 400,000 |
| Jet magazine | Weekly | 1.2 million |
| Sister2Sister | Monthly | 800,000 |

**TELEVISION SHOWS**
106 and Park
Target and local television markets

**KEY EVENTS**
Black Expo                        Essence Festival
                                  Local statewide events

**VIDEO**
Service concept video to MTV, BET, and VH-1 Soul

**MARKETING TOOLS**
| Video | EPK | One-Sheet |
|---|---|---|
| Teaser postcard | Flyers | Postcards |

Custom press kit (Artist, Executive, Photo, Folder)

**Point of Purchase (P.O.P.)**
11x17 artist poster        12x12 flat

**Advertising Materials**
Internet banner ads        TV spots (cut from EPK)

# MARKETING PLAN EXAMPLE

**MARCH**
Press Release/Email Blast: record label signing & distribution deal

**APRIL**
LIVE RECORDING: Press Release/Email Blast

**MAY**
Order promotional paraphernalia listed in Launch Plan
Edited video available

**JUNE**
06/16 : **Advertising Campaign Begins**
Trade magazines for July-October
Internet, etc.
Secure key placement bookings at conferences/festivals

06/24   One-sheet release to retail (incorporated with Retail Promoter)
One-sheet release to radio (incorporated with Radio Promoter)

**JULY**
07/01   Single(s) serviced to radio
Local markets provide single and FREE breakfast w/group to
morning shows and afternoon drive-time shows.

07/07   Radio add date
FREE brunch w/group for radio and distribution company.

TBD     Launch grass roots campaign building up to release on 8/19
Distribute single's and promo items
POP (Point of Purchase) to retail
Radio calls

**AUGUST**
08/19   Album CD release date

**JANUARY**
Soul Train Awards
Vibe Awards

*Marketing plan contributed by Page E. Turner*

# 7.
......................

# How Do I Get My Music on the Radio?

We live in a time when it's especially difficult to get radio airplay for an independent recording project because of the relaxation of FCC regulations, which now allow large conglomerates to own several different stations in any particular market. As a result, most major U.S. radio stations are now owned by large conglomerates that control thousands of radio stations. In most cases, these big companies have one programmer programming all the stations under a specific format that the media conglomerate owns.

## The Radio Station

Radio stations are sites configured for broadcasting sound. Traditionally, stations broadcasted through the air using radio waves, a form of electromagnetic radiation, sent by transmitters and received by antennas. Today many, if not most stations, broadcast via cable FM, local wire networks, satellite, or the Internet, as well as atmospheric broadcasting.

### Program director

The program director is responsible for a station's on-air program, sound, and feel. He determines the station's direction, contests, special events, and promotions, all the while adhering to the station's music format, which is chosen to attract distinct groups of listeners, who, in turn, attract advertisers and sponsors. The program director compiles the weekly play list and decides which records will be added or dropped.

*The "cookie cutter" programming formula*

*The lenient FCC rules that allow large media companies to own radio stations in various markets has caused the homogenizing of popular music. When one program director programs and controls the playlist of hundreds or even thousands of radio stations, it results in programmers whose main concern is Arbitron ratings and bottom-line profits, and they follow cookie-cutter formulas and mostly play records that sound like the last hits.*

### Music director

The music director assists the program director in picking songs to add to the playlist, or drop. He is the liaison with the record label reps, which bring him the week's new music for the station's consideration. The music director researches each song's appeal based on airplay at stations with similar formats in other markets, and recommends to the program director those songs best suited to the station's format.

### Playlist

The playlist is the list of songs being played in a consistent, measurable rotation on radio stations. The list is reported to trade publications to compile charts. The playlist shows the amount of times a record is being played during the week and usually shows activity over the past three weeks. The playlist details how many records are added or dropped in the current week. Most playlists are reported once a week to trade publications.

### Radio add

When radio stations decide to add a record to their playlist, it is referred to as a radio add (not ad, which is short for an advertisement). The station's programming team reports which records have been added and dropped to radio and record industry trade publications and charts. Radio adds are usually scheduled for a specific date, so the label has a few days to prepare the marketplace (making sure product is in the stores, point of purchase materials are displayed, etc.). Record companies would prefer that all stations add a specific record at the same time, which can make the greatest impact on the charts. This also allows for records to be tracked in many markets simultaneously for spins and plays and reported to airplay charts or electronic monitoring systems, such as BDS, to determine a record's activity and the size of audiences exposed to the record.

### Rotation

Rotation refers to how often a record is played. When a record is played consistently, usually more than five times a week, it will be indicated on the radio station's playlist.

### Recurrent

When a record is dropped from a playlist then re-added or played once in a while, it is said to be recurrent.

### Radio single or radio edit

A radio single is a version of the album track that is edited for radio purposes. Radio typically prefers that a single is longer than 3:30 (three minutes, thirty seconds). If the album's original version is longer, the radio station will request an edited or shorter version. Or if the album is unsuitable for a listening audience (i.e., explicit lyrics), the radio station will require a clean or edited version with unsuitable material removed.

### Radio networks

A radio network is a system that distributes radio programming to multiple radio stations. Most radio networks also produce much of their programming.

### How satellite radio works

In 1992, the U.S. Federal Communications Commission (FCC) allocated a spectrum in the "S" band (2.3 GHz) for nationwide broadcasting of satellite-based Digital Audio Radio Service (DARS). Of the four companies that applied for licenses, only two were granted rights to broadcast: Sirius (formerly CD Radio) and XM (formerly American Mobile Radio). Each company has satellites in orbit above the earth to transmit their programming. Programs are beamed to one of the satellites, which then transmit the signals to the ground, where your radio receiver picks up one of the channels within the signal. Signals are also beamed to ground repeaters for listeners in urban areas where the satellite signal can be interrupted. Both providers

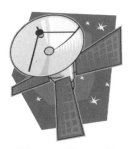

**Why satellite radio?**
*Just as many TV viewers have come to consider cable TV a life necessity, so too is satellite radio becoming a mainstream replacement for traditional AM/FM listening. Yes, you have to pay for it, but like cable, you get way more channels and edgier, more innovative programming. Plus, you don't lose your favorite station as you travel across the state or country. Satellite players show the artist and name of the song— definitely a plus for those who like to know what they're hearing. In the U.S., there are two main players in the satellite radio industry: XM and Sirius.*

have partnered with automobile manufacturers to offer satellite radio in new car models. And each has systems that will search the channels for your favorite music and alert you when and where the songs are playing.

### Digital Music Express (DMX)

Founded in 1992, Digital Music Express is a subscription service that provides 100 channels of music in digital format in two ways: directly via satellite, and more commonly, via cable TV companies. It is available in the U.S. and Canada, and is also offered on some airlines. DMX now faces stiff competition from the next generation of services, such as Sirius and XM Radio, which both deliver their signals directly through small roof-mounted antennas, rather than through a small dish that DMX or Direct TV require. Other companies provide similar services, such as Muzak (with dish, and to businesses only), and Music Choice (via cable TV and DirecTV).

### More on the radio add

The program director is usually a corporate type who programs the stations across the country—every station being owned by the media conglomerate. Adding a record to a national playlist can mean being added to hundreds of stations at once. This can cause a record to "explode"—receive massive national airplay and exposure overnight. Being added to a national playlist is an especially coveted position, which is usually reserved for a select few companies who are in the business of packaging and selling block advertising across their many stations. Because of this, it is extremely difficult for the independent record label to compete because the radio conglomerates are interested solely in companies with large advertising budgets, who can support their artists by sending them around the country to the various markets where these conglomerates own stations.

In some cases, these large conglomerates also own concert venues where they also would like to book the artist. Generally, this is an expense that only major record labels can afford. Besides, the conglomerates are also interested in forming relationships with record labels that are **content providers**, meaning not just **one hit wonders**. They are interested in forging relationships with companies that can consistently provide artists and hit records and tour support for their artists. Consequently, unless you have a lot of money to invest or you're affiliated in some way with a major label such as a joint venture label deal, it's virtually impossible to receive national airplay across the board.

### Radio alternatives

There are some alternatives to mainstream commercial radio, such as the emerging medium of Internet radio. There are tons of Internet or Web radio stations that are more open to playing independent or niche music. There are also digital music services like Music Choice that are more likely to play independent music and have the genres separated for the listener's pleasure. There is also satellite radio. It's much easier to get your music played on these types of stations. College radio stations are another great resource. Many colleges and universities have local radio stations that are programmed by students and they are more likely to play an independent release.

### Nielsen BDS

Nielsen Broadcast Data Systems is the world's leading provider of off-the-air music tracking for the entertainment industry. Employing a patented digital pattern recognition technology, Nielsen BDS captures more than 100 million song detections annually on more than 1,200 radio stations in over 130 markets in the U.S. and Puerto Rico, plus 22 Canadian markets.

Radio formats monitored include Adult Alternative, Adult Contemporary, Album Rock, Classic Rock, Contemporary Christian, Country, Light AC, Modern Rock, Oldies, R&B (including Rap and Hip-Hop), Spanish (including Latin Contemporary, Regional

Mexican and Tropical Salsa), and Top 40. Nielsen BDS also monitors seven U.S. music video channels and nine Canadian video channels.

Executives from record companies, radio stations, publishing firms, performance rights organizations, music retailers, independent promoters, film and TV, and artist management are among those who query more than 10,000 reports daily from Nielsen BDS products: ENcore, BDSRadio.com, BDSexpress.com and BDS RealTime.

Nielsen BDS information is utilized exclusively by *Billboard*, *Airplay Monitor*, and *Canadian Music Network* magazines in determining their radio airplay music charts.

### Arbitron
Arbitron measures how many listeners radio stations have at various times of the day. Radio stations use the information to determine the size of their market share. As a result, stations determine how much they can charge for advertising on the station. Advertising agencies and marketers use Arbitron's radio ratings service to plan more effective radio buys and target consumers more precisely.

### The DJ as artist
A recent phenomenon in the music community (but primarily in popular music) is the idea that some DJs are not simply playing records but are creating new music out of the playback and mixing of the pre-recorded media. Fuelled mainly by the innovative mixing techniques that have come out of the Hip-hop and EDM scenes, and regarded as a musical extension of the literary cut-up technique, the growing attitude is that a DJ is not content simply to beatmatch two or three records and layer them over each other, but that the end product should emerge as a new musical composition. To achieve this goal, such a DJ may employ techniques like phrasing, sampling, scratching, the application of effects (such as delay,

flange, etc.), and any other technique the DJ feels inclined to use. Examples of such DJs as "artists" adding musical or dramatic value include DJ Clue, Kay Slay, and DJ Who Kidd.

### The independent (indie) promoter

The independent promoter is contracted by record companies to work specific records, but he is not a record company employee. Years ago it was common practice for record companies to pay disc jockeys under the table to play certain records, a practice known as *payola*. Payola was outlawed in 1960, after a number of disc jockeys were charged with taking bribes from record companies to play songs.

Since it's now illegal for radio stations to take money directly from record companies in exchange for airplay without announcing it to the listening audience, record companies have found a loophole in the law by using middlemen. Record companies say they're being forced to pay independent promoters, so-called indies. The indies then pay the radio stations, buying access to get the songs heard. And it's all legal.

These independent promoters can charge $50,000 to $80,000 per single and are instrumental in getting records played on mainstream radio. Record labels spend up to $400,000 per album on independent promoters.

### What is payola?

Payola is the paying of cash or gifts in exchange for airplay without announcing that fact to the radio audience. The word "payola" is a contraction of the words "pay" and "Victrola" (LP record player), and entered the English language via the record business. The first court case involving payola was in 1960.

## Major radio players

**Clear Channel** *owns stations in 247 of the nation's 250 largest radio markets. Clear Channel in particular dominates the Top 40 format and controls 60 percent of rock-radio listening.*

**Infinity Broadcasting** *is headquartered in New York City and owns approximately 180 radio stations located in 22 states in the nation's largest markets.*

**Radio One, Inc.** *is the nation's seventh largest radio broadcasting company and the largest company that primarily targets African-American and urban listeners. Radio One owns and/or operates 69 radio stations located in 22 urban markets in the United States and reaches approximately 13 million listeners weekly.*

**Emmis Broadcasting** *owns and operates 23 FM radio stations and 4 AM radio stations in New York City, Chicago, Los Angeles, Phoenix, St. Louis, Indianapolis, and Terre Haute, Indiana.*

On May 9, disc jockey Alan Freed was indicted for accepting $2,500, which he claimed was a token of gratitude and did not affect airplay. He paid a small fine and was released.

Before Alan Freed's indictment, payola was not illegal, but commercial bribery was. After the trial, the anti-payola statute was passed and payola became a misdemeanor, with penalties up to $10,000 in fines and one year in prison.

### Commercial single
The commercial single is a single track from an album that is chosen by the label/artist/manager to be made available for sale at retail accounts. Radio airplay of the commercial single drives consumers to the record stores.

### Radio syndication
Syndication is when a particular show or program is broadcast by several different radio stations in several regional markets simultaneously. It is done electronically, allowing several markets to share the programming costs and to be heard simultaneously across the country.

## Radio Resources

**www.Radio-locator.com** lists radio stations globally, including Internet (Web) radio.

**www.cmj.com** is the website for *CMJ*, the *College Music Journal*. The CMJ Network connects music lovers with the best in new music through print and interactive media, as well as live events.

**www.BillboardRadioMonitor.com** — Stay informed and ahead of the competition with *Billboard Radio Monitor*, online and in print, with the most complete radio business coverage.

**www.musicchoice.com** — Music Choice is available in the U.S. from more than 650 cable systems and includes a wide choice of music formats including Rock, Rap, Gospel, Country, Blues, Jazz, Hip-hop, Classical, and more.

**www.dmxmusic.com** — DMX Music is the global leader in delivering unparalleled personal music experiences via digital cable, satellite, and the Internet to over ten million homes, 180,000 businesses and 30 airlines. A subsidiary of Liberty Media, Inc., DMX Music is heard daily by a worldwide audience of 80 million.

**www.sirius.com** — 120 channels of satellite radio: 65 devoted to commercial-free music, in almost every genre imaginable, plus 55 channels of sports, news, and talk.

**www.XMradio.com** — XM Radio is America's No. 1 satellite radio provider with over 3 million subscribers; 100 percent commercial-free music; 33 channels of news, sports, talk and entertainment; 21 dedicated channels of XM instant traffic and weather; and the deepest playlist in the industry, with access to over 2 million titles.

### Radio sampler
A promotional version or versions of the album's single that is sent to radio stations for airplay, usually done in CD format.

### Radio drop
A radio drop is an announcement on a radio station when a recording artist will be presented at a certain date and time. Often it is recorded by artists when they are in the radio studio, or as one of many radio drops recorded for stations in cities where artists will be touring.

### Air personality (radio personality)
A radio personality announces and introduces records. The personality usually broadcasts during a regular time slot and is a familiar person. A radio personality can be a famous TV personality (such as Ryan Seacrest, KIIS-FM, Los Angeles), a comedian, or even a recording artist.

**A Clear Advantage...**

**43**=number of radio stations owned by Clear Channel Communications before the 1996 Telecommunications Act was passed.

**1,207**=number of radio stations owned by Clear Channel eight years later, in 2004.

# 8.

............

# Royalties: How Do I Get Paid?

The dark secret in the record business is how little artists really make. Most artists spend their careers waiting until the recording costs have been fully paid back (recouped) from their royalties so they can start receiving royalty checks. But if your royalty rate is somewhere between 5 percent and 12 percent of the list price, and you only earn between 80¢ and $2 on every record sold, to pay back your recording costs of, say, $300,000, plus that $100,000 video you needed, you have to sell between 200,000 and 300,000 CDs before you start collecting any artist royalties. So on a million-selling album, your artist royalties may be between $800,000 and $2 million. After paying back the record company, that leaves you with somewhere between $400,000 and $1.6 million.

That's why there's an old record business adage: if you want to make make a million dollars, start with two million dollars and save one. Most artists are never fully recouped—they usually owe money back to the record label for recording costs, to repay their artist advance, and various promotion and marketing charges. Usually, the only money artists ever see from the sales of records is their initial advance against royalties. For these reasons, your lawyer will tell you to get the biggest advance you can, because you may never see any royalty checks.

The good news is that there are other ways to get paid: songwriting and publishing royalties, synch licenses, touring, and using your name to earn more money outside of your recording contract. All these

### Why no artist royalties for public performances?

*Recording artists don't earn royalties on public performances (when their music is played on the radio, on TV, or in bars or restaurants). It is based on copyright law and the fact that when radio stations play your songs, more CDs and tapes are sold.*

*However, songwriters and publishers do earn royalties for public performances, plus a small portion of the recording sales.*

*Artists only earn royalties for "public performances" when their songs are played in digital arenas (like Webcast or satellite radio) and the listener is a subscriber to the service.*

sources kick in after you have that hit record, which by itself may not make you that much money.

### Copyright collective
A copyright collective or copyright collecting agency is a body created under copyright law that is designated to collect royalty payments from various individuals and groups for copyright holders. The collective may have the authority to license works and collect royalties as part of a statutory scheme, or by entering into an agreement with the copyright owner to represent the owner's interests in deals with licensees and potential licensees.

What's my share?

## How much can I make on a platinum (million-selling) album?

*Assuming your recoupable costs are $500,000 (to repay your recording costs, artist advance, and marketing costs, such as your video-clip): If your CD's list price is $16.98, first you pay 25% ($4.25) as a "packaging deduction," which leaves you about $12.74. So if you sell a million units, you earn a gross amount of $1,274,500. From that, deduct the $500,000 recoupable costs (as specified in your contract), which in this case leaves a net amount of $774,500. From there you deduct costs of the professional services and goods YOU hire or buy.*

In the U.S. and Canada, these groups are called performance rights organizations or PROs. Other organizations such as artist rights groups license and collect royalties for the reproduction of paintings of living or recently deceased artists whose work has not yet entered the public domain.

### Performance rights organization (PRO)
These organizations exist to collect and distribute royalties on behalf of audio and video artists for performances of their copyrighted works under copyright law.

### Royalties
Royalties are the monies paid to an artist, producer, or songwriter for their contributions to an artistic work by the record company, publishing company, and performance rights organization.

### Advance
An advance is a portion of the expected royalties paid to the artist, producer, or songwriter before an album is released. This amount is then deducted from future royalties until the original amount of the advance is repaid.

### Pro rata
Pronounced pro **rat**-ah or pro **ray**-tah, pro rata is Latin

# *Where does all the money go?*

**Here's where each dollar from a
$16.98 CD purchase ends up:**

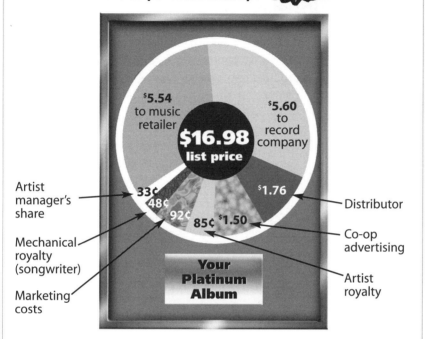

$5.54
to music
retailer

$16.98
list price

$5.60
to
record
company

Artist
manager's
share

33¢

48¢

92¢ 85¢ $1.50

$1.76

Distributor

Mechanical
royalty
(songwriter)

Co-op
advertising

Marketing
costs

**Your
Platinum
Album**

Artist
royalty

| | |
|---|---|
| **$5.54** | The music retailer buys a $16.98 album for about $11.50 and sells it for $16.98, thus earning about $5.48 per album |
| **$5.60** | Record label gets between $5.50-$5.70 per album |
| **$1.76** | Distributor's share is between $1.60-$1.80 |
| **$1.50** | Co-op marketing— for advertising and retail programs like listening stations, newspaper ads. |
| **$0.92** | Marketing—video and other costs listed in your contract |
| **$0.85** | Artist royalty |
| **$0.48** | Artist mechanical royalty (songwriting) |
| **$0.33** | Your manager's share |

*\* All prices are approximate because contracts vary.*

**If you snooze, you lose ...**

*If you want to get paid, you need to pay attention to the money coming in and going out. If it appears that you're asleep at the wheel, that money will disappear. It may be "lost," stolen, invested unwisely, never paid to you in the first place, and spent on things you never wanted. You can bank on it.*

for "in proportion." It refers to the portion to be received or an amount to be paid based upon a percentage share of ownership. Pro rata is used to calculate royalties paid on albums based on the number of songs contributed by different artists and producers.

Basically it means that if you work on a project as an artist or producer, but you are not the sole producer; or if you are a featured artist on a compilation project, your contribution to the project is proportionate to the number of songs on which you participated.

Ten songs per album is the most that record companies pay royalties on. If the contract calls for the label to give 3 percent of royalties to the producer, and there are ten producers, each get one-tenth of the 3 percent. If you do three songs, for example, you'll get three times that amount. This is a very important concept which, unfortunately, most newcomers to the business don't grasp.

For example: if there are ten songs on the album and either the producer or featured artist gets 3 percent for the production, and they've produced all ten of the songs, the producer earns the entire 3 percent. But if the producer produces only one of the ten tracks, he receives one-tenth of 3 percent. The only way to receive the full 3 percent producer royalty is to produce all ten tracks on an album.

Because there is only one 3 percent royalty overall for the entire project, and it's divided according to the percentage of songs the producer produces, if your contract says you are to receive a royalty of 3 percent for your work, it's broken down to ten tracks. So if you produce two out of ten, you actually receive two-tenths of 3 percent. If you produced 3 tracks out of ten you get three-tenths of 3 percent.

# Five Ways to Earn Royalties

| Mechanical Royalties | Performance Royalties | Synch Licenses | Sheet Music | Artist Royalties & Producer Royalties |
|---|---|---|---|---|
|  |  |  |  |  |
| Songwriting royalties, paid by the record label to the publisher, who collects payment on behalf of the writer and publisher. Regulated by the statutory rate. |  Generated by radio and club airplay, paid by performance rights organizations (BMI, ASCAP, SESAC). |  Paid when music is used in movies and television commercials, collected by the music publisher, who issues the synch license. | Paid by the music publisher on every piece of sheet music sold, according to the publishing contract with the songwriter. | A percentage of the CD's sales is paid by the record company according to the artist's recording contract and producer's contract. |

## . . . And even more ways:

**Ring tones:** Licensing your song for usage as a mobile phone ringtone has become a goldmine for artists with big hits.

**Merchandising:** T-shirts, albums, posters, and hats.

**Touring:** owning a piece (percentage) of admissions, net profits, or other sources of tour income.

# Advance and Recoupment

Artist's royalties from
album sales
$100,000

Artist's advance
(against royalties)
$20,000

| Artist gets $20,000 advance | Album earns in artist royalties | $100,000 |
|---|---|---|
| | Recoupment (Artist pays back $20,000 advance) | −20,000 |

### Remainder
### owed to artist: $80,000*

\* *Before the artist receives any royalties, other expenses will be recouped, including recording & marketing costs and various expenses paid for by the label.*

### Catalog

A catalog is the body of master recordings owned by
a label. It's one thing to put out new artists and break
records (i.e., turn records into hits), but the real heart
of the business is the catalog. It's the "meat" of the
business that provides a constant stream of income
year after year. For instance, Motown owns master
recordings by such artists as Boyz II Men, Marvin
Gaye, Stevie Wonder, the Jackson 5, and the Supremes.
These titles can be repackaged into all kinds of
compilations and greatest hits packages and sold
for generations to come. Every ten years a new
generation discovers Bob Marley and the Eagles and
purchases their "evergreen" titles. Catalogs sell with
little or no cost to the record label. This is why ownership of master recordings is vital to the record label: It
pays for breaking new artists.

### Taxes

The number one cause of bankruptcy is taxes. MC
Hammer, TLC, Willie Nelson and other multimillion-
aires showed us how easy it is to forget that the more
money you make, the more you owe the government.
In a very good year, don't be surprised if 40 percent of
your earnings are paid to Uncle Sam as taxes. It is said
that the reason Motown Records survived when
hundreds of other small labels failed in the '50s and
'60s was their brilliant tax attorney, who guided the
company from the day it was founded. If you're lucky,
someday you'll have tax problems, too.

# 9.

# Who Handles the Business?

In the music business, one of the most important decisions you will make is whose advice you will follow. There's an army of experts who can handle every situation that comes up—starting with your manager, who is the overall coordinator of your career activities. You can hire people who make you look good, sound good, feel good, and guide you towards success.

Your accountant or business manager will oversee your budget. A production coordinator keeps everything in line during the recording process. While you're on tour, a small army of experts will handle life on the road. Your booking agent will negotiate your gigs and a promoter will pay and book the venues. Independent firms can be hired by the artist or record company to supplement the label's efforts in the specialized areas of marketing and radio promotions. This chapter is a complete look at the individuals who handle the business.

### Manager (Artist's manager)
The manager serves as a liaison between the record label and the artist, secures endorsements, tour packages, record deals, and protects the interests of the artist.

### Certified Public Accountant (CPA)
CPAs are accountants that have passed the CPA exam developed and graded by the American Institute of CPAs. Only CPAs are allowed to state opinions on financial statements. Many states prohibit those without CPA licenses to call themselves accountants.

## What should I look for in a manager?

*Unfortunately, it's very difficult to attract a good manager unless you are visible, and you can't become visible without a good manager. Which is why many artists start with family members or friends and eventually replace them with those who are more experienced and better connected. Look for a manager who can make things happen for you while keeping your best interests at heart. It's absolutely crucial that your manager totally understand the business and maintain a cool head and good relationships with the record label, attorneys, booking agents, and everyone else in your career, especially during difficult times.*

### How do I find a good lawyer?

*To negotiate your way through the music business, it's crucial to find an attorney that specializes in entertainment or contract law. Try looking on liner notes of your favorite artists' CDs (they often thank their lawyers and list their offices). Remember that most entertainment attorneys are located in the three cities where most of the music industry is based: Los Angeles, New York, and Nashvillle (Country music). If you live outside these areas or lack the resources to hire a high-profile attorney, try your local university. It may have an entertainment law program through which you could get a referral to an attorney.*

### Road crew

Roadies are the technicians who travel on tour with musicians and who handle every part of the production except actually playing the music. This catch-all term covers security people, lighting, sound and instrument technicians, tour manager, set designer, riggers (people who set up wiring), and pyrotechnics technicians, among others.

### Musical director

The musical director—usually a member of the band —is responsible for choosing, assembling, rehearsing, and conducting the band for solo artists or groups that are not musically self sufficient. The musical director is usually hired by the artist's manager or by a record label executive, whether for a national tour, promotional dates, or a television appearance. Musical directors are known to maintain long working relationships with the artist—in most cases lasting throughout the artist's career.

### Publicist

A publicist's job is to inform or influence specific publications or media outlets using writing, marketing, advertising, publicity, promotions, and special events. Some publicists work as full-time employees of record companies, artists, or producers. Others work for public relations firms that contract their services to clients who pay for their expertise at keeping them in or out of the spotlight, whichever is necessary.

### Composer

A composer writes music, usually in a standard type of musical notation, thus allowing others to perform the music. This distinguishes composers from musicians, who improvise. A person may be called a composer without creating written music, since not all musical genres rely on written notation. In this context, the composer is the originator of the music, and usually its first performer. Later performers then repeat the musical composition they have heard.

The term "composer" is often used specifically to mean a composer in the Western tradition of classical music. In popular and folk music, the composer is called a songwriter, since the music generally takes the form of a song.

### Music mogul
A mogul is an important or powerful person who is able to make things happen by utilizing resources of the press, television, and motion pictures. Some examples of modern-day moguls are Clive Davis, Russell Simmons, David Geffen, and Sean "P. Diddy" Combs.

### Business manager
A business manager handles all your money— collecting it, investing it, keeping track of it, paying your taxes and all your other bills.

### Merchandiser
A merchandiser creates a product relating to the recording artist that can be sold at venues where the artist performs, and other places. Merchandisers work closely with concert promoters to make sure each appearance has enough merchandise for fans to purchase. Recording artists receive a percentage of revenue from merchandise sold.

### Intern
An intern is usually an unpaid employee of the record label who works for the experience, connections, and training. His errands may include fetching coffee or tracking airplay at radio stations. Although the job may seem worthless, it has proven to be one of the most effective ways to get an inside glimpse into the music business. Many of today's moguls started as interns, including Sean Puffy Combs and David Geffen.

## What do booking agents do?

*Booking agents book shows for artists and arrange nearly every detail. Lighting, sound, meals, hotel accommodations, transportation and even snack food are all handled by bookers for their artists. For concert buyers, they find the right artist to fit into a gig's needs and budget. Many major booking agents won't represent a client unless they are already with a major label and have national distribution of their music. Because of this, most indie artists do their own booking and generally do not require as many riders (extras)*

### Music supervisor

The music supervisor is responsible for selecting music to be performed. S/he also works closely with musical writers and arrangers to create music and consider existing music that is appropriate for a project, whether it be a commercial, TV program, movie, or other event.

### Product manager

Usually an employee of the record label, the product manager is assigned by the record company to a specific album project. S/he coordinates the efforts of the marketing, promotion, and sales staff to make sure that the efforts of each department mesh with all other departments to increase product sales.

### Road manager

The road manager is responsible for life on the road when an artist is on tour. S/he secures the hotel rooms, supervises soundchecks, and makes sure the artist shows up on time for the performance and promotional appearances in every city.

### Booking agent

A booking agent schedules (books) performances for the artist, secures a contract with the promoter for each date, and negotiates the artist's fee. A good booking agent has good relationships with owners of venues where artists perform. Most booking agents are employed by licensed agencies. Booking agents will usually find you when you begin to get a buzz via word of mouth or a *Billboard* chart position.

### Concert promoter

A concert promoter organizes and stages a concert or event from start to finish. Most of the responsibility and risk falls on the concert promoter, who is in a unique position: he or she stands to make a huge profit if the event is successful, but can lose a fortune if there's too many empty seats. The promoter's most important job is matching the venue to the performer; in other words, finding a venue that has

the highest probability of selling every seat for the
artist's performance.

### Personal trainer

A personal trainer is a fitness professional hired to
help an artist attain exquisite physical condition.
Trainers design custom exercise regimens for artists.
Often, trainers are also dieticians and can develop
healthy meal plans for better eating habits, which
keep artists looking and feeling good.

### Stylist

A stylist is a tastemaker that has become very
important over the past 20 years as the industry
switched to an image-driven business. As a result, the
visual image can be more important that the musical
ability. The stylist—usually hired by the record label
or manager—determines the overall "look" of the
artist, or creates the vibe the artist is trying to
achieve. The stylist can become a great asset by
creating a distinctive, unique look for the music video,
album covers, TV appearances, magazine layouts, and
photo shoots. Stylists oversee hair color, cut, and
style, accessories, and jewelry. They must maintain
a consistent look and capture the attention of
the audience base. Most stylists have working
relationships with designers and the top clothing
manufacturers and are able to get clothes on loan
or even on a gratuity basis in exchange for exposure
in videos and magazine spreads for the designers.
Most stylists have representation or agents and
maintain working relationships with music video
directors and photographers.

### Bodyguard

A bodyguard protects his client from threats and
dangerous situations, including personal assault,
kidnapping, assassination, loss of confidential
information, and from smaller problems: situations
that are potentially embarrassing, belittling,
annoying, time-wasting, or might result in bad
photos. Bodyguards are typically armed and trained

in unarmed combat. But their most important skill is the ability to assess a situation and decide how best to respond to minimize the problem. High profile artists are protected by several bodyguards who work together as a unit, using different vehicles and sometimes decoy vehicles, to protect their client. Lower profile artists may be accompanied by a single bodyguard, who may double as a driver.

# STAGE PLOT

*One of the road manager's duties is to draw a diagram of how the stage should be set up. The stage plot shows the placement of every micro-phone, instrument, monitor, amp, and electrical source. The stage plot is sent to the venue ahead of the show.*

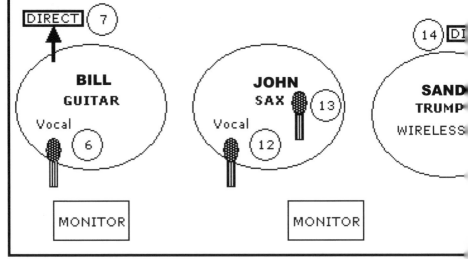

1. Kick
2. Snare
3. Hi Hat
4. Toms

5. Julio Bass
6. Bill Vocal
7. Bill Guitar DI
8. Lesley Front Vocal

Management Contact:

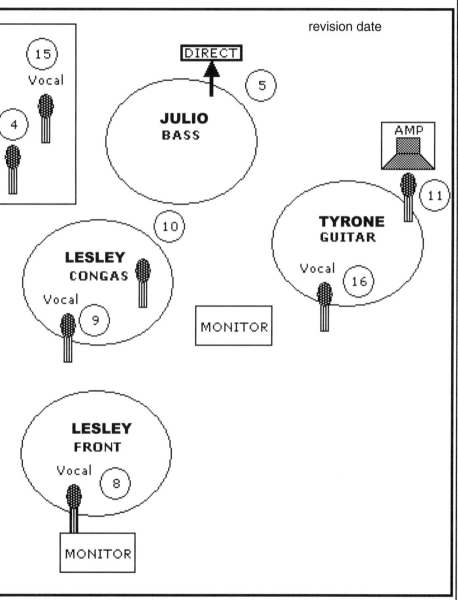

revision date

9. Lesley Congas Vocal
10. Lesley Congas
11. Tyrone Guitar
12. John vocal

13. John Sax
14. Sandy Trumpet
15. Chuck Vocal
16. Tyrone Vocal

# 10.

# How Record Labels Work

A **record label** (record company) specializes in recording, manufacturing, distributing, and promoting audio and video recordings. The name derives from the paper labels with the company's logo and music information placed on the center of phonograph records in the early 20th Century.

Nowadays, the four major major record labels are owned by a few large major media giants that make up almost all of the global market. The music business goes through cycles when large conglomerate companies buy up many smaller labels, which usually leads to an environment where small labels step up to fill the needs of the independent record market niches.

### Independent record label

An independent record label has no affiliation with a major label or major distributor. The independent is self-sufficient and contains its own in-house promotion, marketing, and A&R departments. In some cases, a single person may perform all of these functions. An experienced independent record label knows its customers well and specializes in a particular genre of music or "niche" music. Most indie labels are distributed by independent distributors, or they may distribute themselves through a network of one-stops or wholesalers and through the Internet. Not so long ago, independents were a dying breed with the larger conglomerates swallowing up all the independent record labels that showed potential or promise. But with the recent explosion

*Gold, Platinum, and Diamond Album Certifications*

*The Recording Industry Association of America awards certification based on units sales:*

**Gold album:**
*RIAA certification of 500,000 units.*

**Platinum album:**
*RIAA certification of 1,000,000 units.*

**Diamond album:**
*RIAA certification of 10,000,000 units*

of Hip-hop music, the independent labels are once again becoming a force to be reckoned with.

An independent record label operates outside the sphere of the "major" record labels—the few companies that dominate the recorded music industry in the western hemisphere. The boundaries are often blurred because successful independent record labels are often purchased or otherwise swallowed up as subsidiaries of major labels. Successful indies also earn revenue with international licensing deals and other deals with major record labels.

When independent labels became fashionable in the late 1970s, major labels created what appeared to be "independent" labels, although they were really just facades. These "pseudo" independent labels would sometimes operate independently from the parent company, or they could be created for one artist, or for the purposes of signing artists under different contractual arrangements than those signed to the parent company. **Boutique labels** (also known as **vanity labels**) were also created for bands or for particular record industry identities. In all cases, "independent" was in the eye of the beholder.

### The resurgence of independent labels

In the 1990s, as consumer versions of expensive recording hardware and software entered the market, (such as the Alesis A.D.A.T. and Pro-Tools) more and more home studios cropped up. Along with consumer CD recorders and the Internet, independent labels were back in the limelight once again. They are typically—although not always—artist-owned and focus on making good music, and not necessarily on the business aspect of the industry or making lots of money. For these reasons, independent artists usually receive less radio play and sell fewer CDs than artists signed to major labels. However, they usually have more control over the music and packaging of the released product.

Some independent labels become successful enough that major record companies negotiate contracts to either distribute their music or purchase the label outright.

The four major media giants that dominate the global music market today are EMI, Sony-BMG, Warner, and Universal.

**Universal Music Group (UMG)** is the largest major label in the record industry, with a 23 percent market share. They have some of the world's biggest artists, including Aerosmith, Eminem, Luciano Pavarotti, and U2. Universal Music was originally the music company attached to the Universal Pictures film studio. Its history is long and complex, but the present organization was formed when its owner, Seagram, bought PolyGram and merged it with UMG in 1998. Seagram has since sold UMG to Vivendi.

**Sony BMG Music Entertainment** is the result of a 50/50 joint venture between Sony Music Entertainment (part of Sony) and BMG Entertainment (part of Bertelsmann AG). It includes labels such as Arista, Columbia, Epic, J, RCA Victor, and RCA Records.

**EMI** Electric and Musical Industries Ltd was formed in 1931 from a merger of the UK Columbia Graphophone Company and the Gramophone Company/HMV. In 1955, to replace the loss of its long-established licensing arrangements with RCA Victor and Columbia Records, EMI entered the American market by acquiring Capitol Records.

**Warner Music Group** is a large conglomerate whose labels include Atlantic, Elektra, London, Reprise, Rhino, Warner Music Australia, Word, and Maverick.

# How Recor

PR

## Creative Division

*Responsible for creating hit product.*

### A&R (ARTIST & REPERTOIRE)

The people who find most of the talent signed by the label, and who work with the recording artist to ensure that the result is a winner.

### PRODUCT MANAGEMENT

Timing is everything: Makes sure that all record company processes and plans click in together at the right time.

### ARTIST DEVELOPMENT

Provides special services for artists as needed (Motown was famous for its "finishing school," which taught artists how to appear in public and conduct interviews). Artist develop-ment makes sure that when an artist visits a town on tour, for example, stores there have plenty of records to sell, displays in place, and an itinerary set up for the artist to visit record stores, radio stations, and other local music hangouts.

## Marketing Division

*Responsible for figuring out how to create a demand for the product.*

### SALES

Gets the records into the stores and keeps them there as needed, as sales ebb and flow. The idea is to make as little product as possible so few CDs are returned, yet enough so that stores don't run out.

### MARKETING

Develops displays and contests, packages the artist's image, and creates support materials designed to catch the eye of your target audience.

### PROMOTION

Gets records played on the radio by whatever means are necessary.

# Labels Work

## Administration
Responsible for handling money and contracts.

### BUSINESS AFFAIRS & LEGAL
Drafts, negotiates, and administers all sorts of contract;6 such as artist deals, foreign licensees, pressing plants, distributors, and record clubs. Makes sure company activities are within the law.

### FINANCE
The bean-counters: They track all the money coming in and going out to make sure the company is not spending more than it brings in. Makes sure all appropriate charges are paid by the artists' royalties, such as recordings costs, videos, etc.

### INTERNATIONAL
Coordinates the release of records everywhere in the world outside of the U.S. In other words, this department sells more than half of the label's total products. Based on contracts with each foreign distributor (licensee), the international department supplies master music tapes, artwork for packaging and display materials, and sets up "visits" for artists appearing overseas.

## Distribution Division
*Responsible for meeting the demand for product: for making high-quality product for public consumption; Duplicating CDs, assembling finished product, and creating "parts" that will be used to make CDs in around the world.*

### PRODUCTION
Works with factories to deliver the parts needed to make CDs to fill distributors' orders, including artwork and music masters, and putting finished product together on assembly lines.

# 11.

# Filesharing: Stealing Music?

*Piracy* is the pilfering or stealing of copyrighted material. Due to the recent explosion of illegal file sharing via the Internet, piracy has become rampant. When music is pirated, no one benefits: there are no royalties paid to the artist, songwriter, or record label. This takes away from the amount of resources available to an artist and record company, and gives them less incentive to produce additional material, so everyone loses. Piracy may seem harmless but in the long run it hurts all music lovers.

## Piracy in different forms

Simple piracy is the unauthorized duplication of an original recording for commercial gain without the consent of the rights owner. The packaging of pirate copies is different from the original. Pirate copies are often compilations, such as the mix CDs of a specific artist, or a collection of a specific genre— slow jams, for example.

*Counterfeits* are copied and packaged to resemble the original as closely as possible. The original producer's trademarks and logos are reproduced in order to mislead the consumer into believing that they are buying an original product.

*Bootlegs* are the unauthorized recordings of live or broadcast performances. They are duplicated and sold —often at a premium price—without the permission of the artist, composer, or record company.

**The price of piracy and music theft?**
According to the International Federation of the Phonographic Industry (IFPI), CD piracy climbed 14 percent in 2002 and the global recorded music market fell 7 percent to $32 billion.

### Copyright issues

Anonymous Internet file sharing services (such as Gnutella and Napster) grew in popularity with the proliferation of high speed Internet connections and the relatively small but high-quality MP3 audio format.

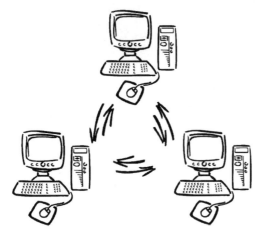

*In peer-to-peer filesharing, there is no central "server" where everyone searches for music. Instead, everyone searches directly through all computer drives connected at the same time.*

### Filesharing software

is used to directly or indirectly transfer files from one computer to another over the Internet. Although file sharing is a legal technology with legal uses, some people (probably the great majority of users) have used it to download copyrighted materials. This has led to attacks against file sharing in general from some copyright owners.

There has been much discussion over perceived and actual legal issues surrounding file-sharing. In circumstances where trading partners are in different countries with different legal codes, there are significant problems to consider. What if a Canadian wishes to share a piece of source code which, if compiled, has encryption capabilities? In some countries, a citizen may not request or receive such information without special permission.

Throughout the early 2000s, the entire filesharing community has been in a state of flux, as record companies tried to shut down as much of it as possible.

**Napster** was the first major file-sharing tool and it popularized filesharing for the masses. It was based on MP3 sharing and was in its original form temporarily shut down by legal attacks from the music industry. It was openly attacked by some artists (notably Dr. Dre, Metallica) and supported by others (Limp Bizkit, Courtney Love, Dave Mathews). Napster was a localized index for MP3 files shared by the users logged into the system. Almost all new, major filesharing software now follows its example in design.

Even though Napster was forced into cooperating against copyright violations, it is an uphill battle since the file-sharing community has flourished and produced many different software systems based on several different underlying protocols.

### Peer-to-peer (P2P)

A P2P network is one that does not rely on dedicated servers for communication, but instead mostly uses direct connections between individuals with computers. The second generation of P2P protocols, such as Limewire, is not as dependent as Napster was on a central server, making it much harder to shut down these systems through court actions. Another strategy is to change the company's organization or country of origin so that it is impossible or useless to attack it through the U.S. justice system.

**Kazaa Media Desktop,** another application commonly used to exchange music files, is widely used to exchange movie files. The official client software can be downloaded free of charge.

### Digital Rights Management (DRM)

Digital rights management or digital restrictions

**Top Music Download Sites**

Apple's iTunes store
AudioLunchBox
eMusic
MP3Tunes
MSN Music
Napster
Sony's Connect
Rhapsody
Virgin Digital
Wal-Mart Music
Downloads Store

management, is an umbrella term for several arrangements by which the usage of a copyrighted digital work can be restricted by the owner of the rights to the work.

### Online audio store

An online audio store is an Internet service that sells audio, primarily music, on a per-song or subscription basis. The realization of the market for these services grew widespread around the time of Napster. Some services have *tethered* downloads, meaning that playing songs requires an active membership.

***iTunes Music Store (iTMS)*** The iTunes Music Store is a paid online music service run by Apple Computer, introduced on April 28, 2003. Within two years, it had sold more than half a billion legal, paid music downloads, making it the No. 1 music download store in the world.

***iPod*** is a hard-drive-based music player from Apple Computer that can play MP3s, MP4a, WAV, AAC, and AIFF files. iPods are distinguished by their small size, simple user interface based on a central scroll wheel, and fast FireWire connections capable of 400 Mbit/sec data transfers. iPods can also used as external hard drives. As of January 2004, the iPod was the most popular digital music player in the United States, with over 50 percent of the market.

# Resources

## DISTRIBUTORS

101 DISTRIBUTION
2375 East Camelback Rd.
5th floor
Phoenix, AZ 85016
1-866-357-3288 or 602-357-3288
Fax 602.357.3288web: www.101distri-
bution.com
Styles/Specialties: all style

AEC ONE STOP
42250 Coral Ridge Dr.
Coral Springs, FL 33065
800-329-7664
Web: www.ant.com
Styles/Specialties: all styles

AFRICAN RECORD CENTRE
DISTRIBUTORS
1194 Nostrand Ave.
Brooklyn, NY 11225
718-493-4500 fax718-467-0099
Contact: Robert Thomas
Styles/Specialties: African, world

ALTERNATIVE DISTRIBUTION
ALLIANCE (ADA)
3400 W. Olive Ave. 6th Floor.
Burbank, CA. 91505
800-239-3232 Fax 818-841-4470
Contact: Bill Kennedy
Styles/Specialties: all styles, especially
college/alternative music
*additional offices in MN & NY

ALLEGRO CORPORATION
14134 NE Airport Way
Portland, OR 97230-3443
1-800-288-2007 Fax 503-257-9061
Web: www. allegro- music. com
Styles/Specialties: jazz, pop, world,
classical and more.

ANTILLA RECORD DISTRIBUTORS
661 10th Ave.
New York, NY 10036
212-582-4546 Fax 212-977-7581
Styles/Specialties: Latin

AROUND THE WORLD
17298 Braxton St.
Granada Hills, CA. 91344
818-360-8088 Fax 818-366-8353
Contact: Bob Weiss
Styles/Specialties: all styles except
hip-hop and heavy metal

ARROW DISTRIBUTING COMPANY
11012 Aurora-Hudson Rd.
Streetsboro, OH 44241
330-528-0405 Fax 330-528-0423

CAROLINE DISTRIBUTION
104 W. 29th St., 4th Flr.
New York, NY10001
212-866-7500 Fax 212-643-5563
E-mail: distribution @ caroline. com
Web: www.caroline.com
Styles/Specialties: indie, punk, dance,
urban, metal.

CENTRAL SOUTH MUSIC SALES
3730 Vulcan Dr.
Nashville, TN 37211
615-8335960 Fax 615-3319417
Styles/Specialties: Christian, gospel

CITY HALL RECORDS
101 Glacier Point, Ste. C
San Rafael, CA 94901
415-457-9080 Fax 415-457-0780
Styles/Specialties: all styles

ENTERTAINMENT DISTRIBUTING INC.
P.O. Box 22738
Eugene, OR 97402
541-484-7070Fax 541-484-7188
Contact: Steve Kugle
Styles/Specialties: all styles

GROOVE DISTRIBUTION
1164 N. Milwaukee Ave.
Chicago, IL 60622
773-435-0250 Fax 773-435-0252
Styles/Specialties: jazzy, deep dance
music

MUSICWEB
P. O. Box 642
Slingerlands, NY 12159
518-469-7654
Styles/Specialties: Wholesaler of
domestic
& imported closeouts and overstocks;
retailer of al major & independent
releases

NAVARRE CORP.
7400 49th Ave. N.
New Hope, MN 55428
763-535-8333 Fax 763-533-2156
Web: www.navarre.com
Styles/Specialties: all styles

NORWALK DISTRIBUTION
1193knollwood Ct.
Anaheim, CA 92801
714-995-8111 Fax714-99590423
Contact: Jimmy White
Styles/Specialties: all styles

ROCK BOTTOM DISTRIBUTION
3400 Corporate Way, Ste. G
Duluth, GA 30096
770-814-8868 Fax 770-497-9206
Styles/Specialties: all styles

RED MUSIC DISTRIBUTION
79 5th Ave.
New York, NY 10003
211-404-0600
Contact: Product Development
Styles/Specialties: all styles
*Additional locations in CA, IL, GA

RYKO DISTRIBUTION
550 W. 25th St. 5th Floor
New York, NY 10001
212-287-6100
Web: www.rykodisc.com
Styles/Specialties: all styles

SIDESTREET DISTRIBUTION
1100 N. Washington
Lansing, MI 48906 USA
800-315-6369 or 517-372-7888
Fax 517-334-5856
Styles/Specialties: folk, bluegrass,
old-time, Celtic, blues, roots and related genres

SONY/BMG MUSIC ENTERTAINMENT
1540 Broadway, 33rd Floor
New York, NY 10036
212-930-4000   Fax 212-930-4398
Web: www.bmg.com
Styles/Specialties: all styles

UNIVERSAL MUSIC & VIDEO
DISTRIBUTION
10 Universal City Plaza, Ste. 400
Universal City, CA 91608
818-777-4400
Web: www.umvd.com
Styles/Specialties: all styles

WEA
111 N. Hollywood Way
Burbank, CA 91505
818-843-6311 Fax 818-840-6212

## RACK JOBBERS

Anderson Merchandisers
(Services 1800 Wal-Mart Stores)
(806) 376-6251
421 E. 34th Street
Amarillo, TX 79103

Handleman Company
(Over 1.3 Billion in annual Sales,
Accounts for more than 11% All
Music sold in the U.S. Services 4,000
Retail Accounts Including K-mart,
Wal-mart)
(248) 362-4400
500 Kirts Bvld.
Troy, MI 48084

## MASS MERCHANTS

Best Buy
(600 + Stores)
(612) 291-1000
7601 Penn Ave. South
Richfield, Mn 55423

Target
(900 + stores)
(612) 696-7500
33 south Sixth street
Minneapolis, Mn 55402

Circuit City
(600 + stores)
(804) 527-4017
9950 Maryland Dr.
Richmond, VA 23233

## NATIONAL CHAINS

Trans World Entertainment Corp.
(1,000 + Stores, Including Coconuts,
Record Town, Camelot and the Wall)
(518) 452-1242
38 Corporate Circle
Albany, New York 12203

The MusicLand Group
(1,000 + stores including Sam Goody
and Media Play)
(952) 931-8800
10400 Yellow Circle Dr.
Minnetonka, MN 55343
Borders Group, Inc.
100 Phoenix Drive
Ann Arbor, MI 48108
734.477.1100

Small and independent music labels
may also soon find their product on
Borders shelves. Here are some ways
to submit your product for
consideration.

If you would like your music stocked
in a Borders store, please send two
copies of each recording and a cover
letter, including company address,
distribution channels and proposed
terms to:

New Vendor Acquisitions
Borders Group, Inc.
100 Phoenix Dr.
Ann Arbor, MI 48108

## ONE STOPS

AEC One Stop Group
(800) 329-7664
4250 Coral Ridge, Fl 33065

## ORGANIZATIONS
### you should know about

AFIM (Association for Independent music)
PO Box 988
Whlitesburge, KY 41858
606-633-0946 Telephone
606-633-1160 Facsimile
www afim.org

AFTRA (American Federation of TV and Radio Artists)
5757 Wilshire Blvd. 9th floor
Los Angeles, CA. 90036
323-634-8100 Telephone
323-634-8147 Facsimile
www. aftra.org

AF of M (American Federation of Musicians)
1501 Broadway
New York, NY 10036
212-869-1330 Telephone
212-764-6134 Facsimile
www.afm.org

AMRA (American Mechanical Rights Agency)
1888 Century Park East Suite 222
Los Angeles, CA 90067
310-843-9546 Telephone
310-8429549 Facsimile
www.amermechrights.com

ASCAP (American Society of Composers, Authors and Publishers)
One Lincoln Plaza
New York, NY 10023
212-621-6000 Telephone
212-724-9064 Facsimile
www.ascap.com

BMI (Broadcast Music Inc.)
320 W. 57th St.
New York, NY 10019
212-586-2000 Telephone
212-246-2163 Fascimile
www.bmi.com

SESAC
55 Music Sq. E
Nashville, TN 37203
615-320-0055 Telephone
615-231-6290 Facsimile

NARAS (National Academy of Recording Arts & Sciences)
3402 Pico Blvd.
Santa Monica, CA 90405
310-392-3777 Telephone
310-392-9262 Facsimile
www.grammy.com

National Association of Composers-USA
PO Box 49256
Barrington Station
Los Angeles, CA 90049
310-541-8213 Telephone
310-373-3244 Facsimile
www.thebook.com/NACusa

RIAA (Recording Industry Assoc. of America)
1130 Connecticut Ave. NW Suite 300
Washington, DC 20036
202-775-0101 Telephone
202-775-7253 Facsimile
www.riaa.com

Recording Artists' Coalition
9903 Santa Monica Blvd., Suite 343
Beverly Hills, CA 90212
Phone: 800-841-9113
Fax: 800-847-3616

Songwriters Guild of America
1500 Harbor Blvd
Weehawken, NJ 70870
201-867-7603 Telephone
201-867-7535 Facsimile
www.songwriters.org

SoundScan
1 N Lexington Ave. 14th floor
White Plains, NY 10601
914-328-9100 Telephone
914-328-0234 Facsimile
www.home.soundscan.com

Uniform Code Council
(To obtain a Barcode)
7887 Washington Village Drive,
Suite 300
Dayton, OH 45459-8605
800 543-8137 (tel)
937 435-3870 (tel)
937 435-7317 (fax)

## DISK & TAPE MANUFACTURERS

ALSHIRE CUSTOM SERVICE
1015 W. Isabel St.
Burbank, CA 91506
800 423-2936 or 818843-6792
Fax 818 569-3718

CINRAM- IVY HILL
250 Park Ave. S., 8th Flr.
New York, NY 10003
646 834-1500 Fax 646 834-1580

DISC MAKERS
3445 Cahuenga Bvld. W.
Los Angeles, CA 90068
800 731-8009 or 323 876-1411
Fax 323 876-6724

DISCUSA
2800 Summit Ave.
Plano TX 75074
800 929-8100 972 881-8800
Fax 972 881-8500

EUROPADISK, LTD.
24-02 Queens Plaza S.
Long Isaland City, NY 11101
718 407-7300 800 455-8555

IMPERIAL TAPE COMPANY
1928 14th St.
Santa Monica, CA 904040
800 736-8273, 310 396-2008
www.nutunes.com

NATIONAL TAPE & DISC CORP.
1100 48th Ave. N
Nashville, TN 37209
800 874-4174 or 615 244-2180
Fax 615 244-7031

OASIS CD MANUFACTURING
12625 Lee Hwy Box 214
Sperryville, VA 22740

RAINBO RECORDS
1738 Berkeley ST.
Santa Monica, CA 90404
310 829-3476 Fax 310 828-8765

SONY DADC
800 358-7316

TAPE SPECIALTY, INC.
24831 Ave. Tibbitts
Valencia, CA 91355
661- 702-9030 or 800 310-0800
Fax 661 702-9029

TECHNICOLOR
623 Welsh Run Rd.
Ruckerville, VA 22963
800 782-0778

WORLD MEDIA GROUP, INC.
6737 E. 30th ST.
Indianapolis, IN 46219
317 549-8484
Fax 317 549-8480
www.worldmediagroup.com

## MASTERING STUDIOS

CAPITOL MASTERING
1750 N. Vine St.
Los Angeles, CA 90028
323 871-5003
Fax 3223 871-5008

FUTURE DISC SYSTEM INC.
3475 Cahuenga Bvld W.
Hollywood, CA 90068
323 876-8733
Fax 323 876-8143

BERNIE GRUNDMAN MASTERING
1640 N. Gower st.
Hollywood, CA 90028
323 465-6264
Fax 323 456- 8367

MARCUSSSEN MASTERING
1545 N. Wilcox Ave.
Hollywood, CA 90028
323 463-5300
Fax 323 463-5600

PRECISION MASTERING
1008 N. Cole AVE.
Hollywood, CA 90038
323 464-1008

STERLING SOUND
88 Tenth Avenue
6th Floor West
New York, NY 10011
Phone: 212-604-9433
Fax: 212-604-9964

# INDEX

# Quick Order Form

**Online orders:** www.swervepublishing.com
**Postal orders:** Swerve Publishing LLC
2118 Wilshire Blvd., Suite 1040
Santa Monica, CA 90403

**Name:**_____

**Address:**_____

_____

**City:**_____

**State:**_____ **Zip:**_____

**Telephone:**_____

**Email:**_____

**Price per book:** $19.95

**Add Shipping & Handling:**

**U.S.** $4 for the first book and $2 for each additional book.

**International:** $9 for first book and $5 for each additional book

**Payment :**  Check__  Visa__  MC__  Optima__  AMEX__  Dis__

Card Number:_____

Name on Card:_____

Exp. Date:_____